RESEARCH IN EDUCATIONAL SETTINGS

**Applied Social Research Methods Series
Volume 29**

APPLIED SOCIAL RESEARCH
METHODS SERIES

Series Editors:
LEONARD BICKMAN, Peabody College, Vanderbilt University, Nashville
DEBRA J. ROG, Vanderbilt University, Washington, DC

RESEARCH IN EDUCATIONAL SETTINGS

Geoffrey Maruyama
Stanley Deno

Applied Social Research Methods Series
Volume 29

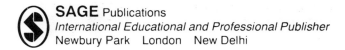

SAGE Publications
International Educational and Professional Publisher
Newbury Park   London   New Delhi

For information address:

SAGE Publications, Inc.
2455 Teller Road
Newbury Park, California 91320

SAGE Publications Ltd.
6 Bonhill Street
London EC2A 4PU
United Kingdom

SAGE Publications India Pvt. Ltd.
M-32 Market
Greater Kailash I
New Delhi 110 048 India

Printed in the United States of America

Library of Congress Cataloging-in-Publication Data

Maruyama, Geoffrey.
    Research in educational settings / Geoffrey Maruyama, Stanley Deno.
        p.   cm. — (Applied social research methods series; 29)
    Includes bibliographical references (p.) and index.
    ISBN 0-8039-4207-9 (c) 0-8039-4208-7 (p)
    1. Education — Research — United States. 2. Education —
    Research — United States — Methodology. I. Deno, Stanley
    II. Title. III. Series.
    LB1028.25.U6M37   1992
    370'.7'0873 — dc20   92-5524
                                                                  CIP

92 93 94 95 10 9 8 7 6 5 4 3 2 1

Sage Production Editor: Judith L. Hunter

Contents

Preface

In keeping with current cultural practices, we should perhaps title this section "ReadMe.1st," for we hope that our readers do not decide that prefaces are irrelevant and skip this one. This section of the book is intended to prepare readers for the chapters that follow. Here we will try to provide readers with an understanding of (a) our objectives in writing this book and how we have chosen to approach those objectives, (b) the assumptions and beliefs that underlie our thinking, and finally, (c) how the book is organized.

This book is primarily intended to help prospective and inexperienced educational researchers to think carefully about a range of important issues as they make plans for conducting research in schools (K-12). The discussion complements traditional research methods texts by focusing on particulars of educational settings and dealing with the types of practical problems that one inevitably encounters in field research. We have oriented this book to persons like ourselves who come into the schools from the outside. At the same time, however, we recognize that many graduate students in education are also teachers, and therefore both insiders and outsiders. We hope that those individuals can help others to gain a better understanding of the dynamics of schools.

As we reflected upon our experiences conducting school-based research, we realized that initially we were unprepared for and surprised by the number and types of nuisances and practical problems that we encountered in our research. We also realized that many issues and problems never seem to be addressed in journal articles, yet appear with some regularity. They can produce sleepless nights for researchers worrying if they can complete their studies without the research losing its meaningfulness and whether their colleagues have experienced similar problems. We believe that problems commonly occur, but are kept hidden from fear of cluttering reports and distracting readers from the substance of the empirical research. Discussion of the problems is relegated to footnotes or deleted in the final draft of reports, journal articles, and books. Many journal editors ask authors to prune coverage of work that could not be done, analyses that could not be conducted, and other problems, unless the information contributes to explaining concepts at issue, data that were collected, or analyses that were performed. Researchers themselves may omit describing their faux pas to avoid appearing careless or, even worse, incompetent. As a result, written reports often are stripped of the headaches and nuisances that appear and must be dealt with even in the most carefully designed research projects.

Because so little is written about pitfalls and pratfalls, in this book we rely more on our own experiences and those of our colleagues for illustrations than we might like. Of necessity the book takes on a personal flavor. We hope, however, that researchers using this book will add to it their own anecdotes to enrich the breadth of experiences that are represented—and share their best stories with us!

We have tried to take a practical approach in addressing issues of research in educational settings. We organized the book to reflect the sequence of activities and concerns that educational researchers commonly encounter. To make the practicalities clearer, we follow a sample research project through the book. Finally, we have added exercises to stimulate discussion about important issues of educational research and to help readers to think about their assumptions about what schools and research are all about.

In looking back over this book, we realized that in writing it we had uncovered a number of assumptions and beliefs underlying our thinking. To help readers understand better the perspective that we have taken, we decided to list the most important assumptions here:

1. Current interest in educational research is very high in academia. Schools have recently received a lot of publicity about their shortcomings (see, e.g., Shapiro, 1991), which has encouraged academic researchers who pride themselves on their abilities as innovators and problem solvers to try their hand at educational research; many of them have little experience conducting research in schools.

2. Schools are poor sites for research unrelated to education. As readers of this book will realize if they haven't before now, there are not many schoolchildren just sitting around waiting for educational researchers to stir them from their doldrums. School days are already very busy and short of time for accomplishing as much learning as is needed.

3. Few teachers eagerly welcome research. Teacher-training programs do not train teachers to consider participating in research as an integral part of their job. A majority of teachers graduate from private colleges or public institutions that began as "normal schools," became teachers' colleges, and now often have changed into state colleges or universities, but still maintain teacher training as a major function. In both types of institutions, the main roles and job expectations for faculty have been to be teachers and advisers, with little emphasis on research. Furthermore, even at major research universities where current role expectations usually include conducting empirical research, many senior faculty were hired more as teacher educators than as researchers. Thus, participating in the designing and conducting of research has not been a typical part of most teachers' professional training.

4. Successful educational research depends on involved and committed insiders. If school staff members do not take some ownership of the research, researchers will find problems in getting interventions implemented and measures collected.

5. Educational researchers need to be flexible and willing to live with less than ideal conditions as well as creative in their data collection and analysis techniques. Unfortunately, neat, tidy, clean experimental designs just don't typically present themselves in school research. There are too many uncontrolled complicating factors, three of which appear as the following points.

6. Sample size inevitably fluctuates over time and sample attrition likely will be high. Schools face turnover and absenteeism; as will be explained later, problems likely will be exacerbated in lower-income schools.

7. Obstacles to research will appear. Obstacles will vary from place to place and time to time, but there will be some. No single study should experience all the problems we describe in this book.

8. Educational researchers have little control over school schedules and school personnel. Researchers must react to circumstances rather than designing them.

9. As the above points should illustrate, educational research is difficult and very time consuming. This area of research can be daunting for junior faculty and graduate students, for progress will likely be slow.

10. Researchers in other fields often underestimate the amount of work involved in good educational research and fail to appreciate it. The cost-benefit balance for young researchers' careers warrants careful consideration before undertaking research in education.

11. Educational research can be very frustrating. In any research, there is always the possibility that the study might not work and all your careful effort will be wasted. Further, the things that keep your study from working may be outside your control.

12. There is a human side to educational research that can markedly affect the research that is conducted. Researchers working with cute, fun, smart kids, and seeing them, for example, not succeeding or becoming frustrated and upset, likely will experience pressure to change the research, even if the failures occur in the "control" conditions. Further, the threshold of teachers for allowing their students to fail is likely even below that of researchers, who are relatively infrequent visitors to classrooms.

We begin Chapter 1 assuming that readers are just beginning to think about doing research in schools, then focus on issues of access and credibility in chapters 2 and 3. In Chapter 4 we move to more traditional issues of designing the research. In chapters 5 and 6 we examine issues that emerge as the design is imposed on the school culture and setting. In particular, we focus on school staff and student assessment. Chapter 7 is focused on issues related to the duration of the study, and Chapter 8 on issues that emerge during implementation. Finally, in Chapter 9 we review what happens after the data are all collected.

For now, we have two additional thoughts to share. First, we realized as we developed this book that in our research we had always tried to roll with the punches, dealing with each crisis as it occurred and only peripherally aware of a patterning and regularity of crises that may be a common part of educational research. Thus, writing this book was educational for us, for it gave us a chance to reflect on and discuss in a systematic way the crazy things that have happened to us. We expect that our reflections and writings will help us to prepare differently in the future. Second, we decided from the start that we would have fun in writing this book, and we did. We hope that you, our readers, enjoy it as well.

EXERCISE

NOTE: We believe that the best way to benefit from most of the exercises is initially to think about them and work through them individually, and then to discuss them with classmates, first in small groups (three to four persons) and then with the whole class. We have found small-group activities most beneficial when the groups are instructed to produce a clearly defined product. For example, in this exercise the product could be to compare and contrast in writing three different viewpoints presented by individuals in the group.

1. *Images of Schools.* Consider what the images are that come to mind for you when you think of school. Think of early elementary grades, later elementary grades, middle school/junior high years, and high school years. Focus on your images of issues that seem important and interesting, including but not restricted to class size, teacher characteristics (e.g., gender, age, race/ethnicity), principal, teacher style (e.g., discipline, method of instruction, encouragement strategies), instructional materials (texts, worksheets), school setting, school size, facilities, public and private schools, rivalries with other schools, student demographics (e.g., ages included in school, racial/ethnic backgrounds, social class of schools). Most important in this exercise is to think about the factors that have formed your images of school.

Acknowledgments

We would like to thank a number of others who have enriched this book through their behaviors and ideas. First, former students Christine Espin and Caryn Cohen worked with us on our study of low-achieving children; they did much of the on-site data collection, kept in touch with the building-level project coordinators, and participated in all the spur-of-the-moment decisions that we were forced to make. Second, numerous colleagues have generously shared their experiences and anecdotes with us; because most of them plan to continue to work in schools, we will let them remain anonymous (see the discussion of stigma in Chapter 1). Third, we are grateful for the research support provided in grant G008730255-89 from the U.S. Department of Education, Office of Special Education and Rehabilitation Services; that grant funded many of the experiences that are described in this book. Fourth, we appreciate cooperation we have received from the Minnesota Department of Education. Fifth, we are appreciative of the efforts of the series editors, Debra Rog and Len Bickman; two anonymous reviewers who forced us to sharpen our ideas and writings; and our Sage editor, C. Deborah Laughton. Finally, no acknowledgments can be complete without including our academic mentors and our families, who, respectively, led us into our profession and kept us relatively happy and productive long enough to complete this book.

1

Educational Research: What an Interesting Idea

So you're planning a research project and are having trouble getting subjects. There is always a subject pool available in the introductory psychology class, but it can be difficult to get access to it. The subjects often have been "contaminated" by other studies that have made them "experiment wise," that is, curious, helpful, skeptical, or resistant. They may not be very representative of the populations about which you are interested (e.g., the pool will not contain many high school dropouts). And you were thinking bigger. You want to conduct a study with a large sample. You want the subjects to react normally and naturally. Where could you go? Ah ha, you think you've got it. Schoolchildren. There are thousands of them. They must have time on their hands (after all, who needs recess) and would probably welcome the opportunity to contribute to science and, coincidentally, to your career development. After getting over your envy of friends who study and work at universities in large cities where there are even more children in schools, you decide to prepare a research project that can be done in schools.

As you sit back and imagine the possibilities, ideas drift through your mind. Classes each with 25 to 30 subjects held captive for 6½ hours per day or more. Talk about availability! School files, filled with information about home addresses; parents' occupations; the students' past performance, ability level, attendance, and so on. Adult raters (otherwise called teachers), who observe the children every day and could tell you all kinds of things about each child. Plus, if you get there first, the students will be naive subjects unskilled in the ways of research. The possibilities seem almost endless. Why didn't you think of this before?

Further reflection shakes you from your reverie. Your unusual creativity notwithstanding, you realize that others before you have probably thought of doing educational research. After all, schools have been around for as long as you remember. As you think about schools and research, your thoughts start drifting back to those good old days when you were a student. Did researchers work in your classes? No? Well, maybe there weren't any. Or they were unobtrusive (Exercise 2, at the end of this chapter, will direct you to think more systematically about research that you might remember). Perhaps the researchers were there, but were such an everyday part of schools that you didn't separate them from other aspects of school and didn't pay attention to them (again, probably not, but it's possible). If they were there, how might they have altered your educational experiences?

Without consciously trying to alter your focus, you find yourself becoming practical, thinking about what people might want to accomplish through research in educational settings, and what educational research actually is. Such thinking brings researchers to questions like: Should the research be primarily theoretical, with its main goal to extend the researcher's thinking and contribute to scientific knowledge? Should it primarily serve school effectiveness, with its main goal to help school officials to make decisions? Even though from our perspective the two preceding questions do not necessarily define mutually exclusive approaches, they may reflect very different orientations to research. Cronbach and Suppes (1969), for example, drew a similar distinction between what they called "decision-oriented" studies, which have as their goal to provide information for a decision maker, and "conclusion-oriented" studies, which follow the interests of the investigator. Decision-oriented research seems to fit more with a view of evaluation-oriented research in which theory is less important than practical problem solving ("Does it work?" is more important than "Why does it work?"). Conclusion-oriented research seems to range from developing basic theory to applied and nontheoretical research where the goal is to produce supportable generalizations about people in social situations, depending upon the interests and bent of the investigator.

As we attempted to determine whether in our own research we have thought or cared more about one type or the other, we encountered a tension. That tension arises from balancing issues of theory development with issues of practice and effectiveness. Some researchers say, "Who cares why it works. It works, and that is what is important"; others counter, "If you don't know why it works and don't have a theoretical basis for understanding its working, it is not much good." What keeps tension around the issue is that there is no single right answer; society needs both people who make programs work and others who can explain why they work. We believe it is shortsighted to argue only for a single type of approach. Theoretically oriented researchers may not be able to solve certain problems until practical work directs their thinking toward explaining a discovered pattern of program outcomes, but practically oriented researchers who may not understand why their intervention worked will have a difficult time transferring a program successfully from one setting to another until a theoretical framework is provided that provides an explanation for the success of the intervention.

As you continue to reflect about educational research, you may think about the various stakeholders in educational research and what their interests and needs are. Consider the researchers at colleges of education at major research universities, who must have a number of important theoretical questions, both basic and applied, that interested them. Consider the people working in schools, like school administrators, who need information in order to set up effective programs, and teachers, who need to be able to select effective teaching techniques and materials. Finally, consider the families, parents and children who want to feel good about and understand the education their schools are providing. In fact, research conducted in educational settings can and should serve the interests of all these groups. On balance educational research needs to achieve a number of purposes, meeting the theory development goals of academic researchers, the practical needs of school personnel, and the information needs of the general public. At the same time, any individual study may focus primarily on one of the purposes. Thus, there can be great variability between studies that fall under the umbrella of educational research.

The primary distinguishing feature of educational research is that it takes place in an applied research setting called a school. (Analogue studies that simulate school environments may take place outside of schools, yet still legitimately be called educational research.) The nature of the research setting is an important feature that should not be underestimated, for it moves researchers away from the academic culture with which they are generally familiar to a different culture with very different values and norms (see, e.g., Boyer, 1983; Goodlad, 1984).

Now that we have raised the issue of culture, we will change our focus temporarily to look broadly at the school environment. Most important, researchers need to recognize that schools each have their own cultures, value systems, norms, and beliefs. Some may be much like the ones that readers of this book remember, but others may produce culture shocks (see, e.g., Shulman, 1990). As outsiders, part of the challenge to us as researchers is to determine how the school culture operates; if we do not understand the school environment in which we are working, we are likely to have difficulty implementing our study. In addition, certain types of school cultures may not be well suited for the types of research we want to do; we can save ourselves much effort by discovering that fact before we begin our project. To illustrate issues that need to be investigated in order to gain an understanding of the culture of schools, take for example norms or rules. Before beginning a research project, it is helpful to know what the rules and expectations are within the school. To discover what the explicit and implicit norms are that guide the behavior of students and teachers in your schools, you might ask questions like: Do most of the students expect to attend college? Do they want to be in school, or are they fighting against what is going on? What is expected and appropriate behavior for students and teachers? How are students treated by the staff? Do teachers have a sense of camaraderie with each other and take pride in their school? Are teachers committed to the curriculum that they are using? Is there tension between different groups of students, or staff, or between teachers and administrators? What kind of leader is the principal? Grasping the essentials of the culture of the school is an important part of beginning to work in school settings.

CASE EXAMPLE

Here we introduce a research problem we will use repeatedly throughout this book for illustration. Imagine that a problem that interests you is whether students who fall behind their peers in school are being given opportunities to catch up to them. You decide to pursue that topic both because it intrigues you and because it happens to be of practical interest to individual students and their parents, and also to schools as a whole. You wonder if those students ever catch up, and, if so, the proportion that catches up, when they catch up, and how the catching up occurs. Although the work is applied and problem oriented, as a researcher you still will need to bring to the problem a number of conceptual perspectives to guide your thinking and, subsequently, your design. Thus, you need to focus on conceptual perspectives that might be relevant. Further, as a broadly focused social scientist, you realize that schooling is more that just good grades, so you decide to broaden the domain of outcome measures, looking at students' personality, aspirations, and popularity as well as their achievement.

You have a general problem to address, but you lack specifics. The problem is very broad and could be addressed in many ways. As a neophyte, you may not be sure where to begin or what to do, let alone what has already been done. But a fortuitous glance at the local news in your newspaper lights on an article on special education programs serving low-achieving children. The article raises the question whether low-achieving students are better served in the regular classroom than in special separate programs that are designed specifically for them and taught by special teachers. What a break! You can focus your concerns on a more finite problem that still bears on the question that interested you, but that looks at the impact of specific curricular decisions on the children. Further, you have a ready-made hypothesis, namely, that students served in regular classes will perform differently (do better or worse) than those served in separate, homogeneous special education classes (see Exercise 3).

To illustrate the process of hypothesis generation, we will provide examples of different perspectives that actually yield inconsistent and competing predictions. First, if you derive your hypotheses from theory regarding the impacts of social stratification and stigma, you could predict *better* performance by students with mild disabilities in regular classrooms, for the regular classroom should contain fewer cues and labels that stigmatize students who are performing poorly (see Hobbs, 1975). The students should be less likely to view themselves as failures and incompetent. (This argument is often used to support "mainstreaming," or educating children who are low achieving or disabled in the "least restrictive" environment possible.) Second, if you derive your hypotheses from the probable impacts of classroom structure on student perceptions and attitudes, you could predict that low-achieving and mildly disabled students might do *better or worse,* depending, for example, upon how effectively the students are integrated into the classroom and whether or not it is cooperative, competitive, or individualistic in structure (see Johnson, Johnson, & Maruyama, 1983). In other words, your predictions would be based on general class climate and patterns of peer relationships. Third, if you base your hypothesis on teacher competence and believe that regular classroom teachers are already overworked and therefore ill equipped to deal with additional, special problems, you could predict a *worse* outcome. Some recent evidence suggests that reading teachers spend less time working with slow readers than they do with other students (see O'Sullivan, Ysseldyke, Christenson, &

Thurlow, 1990), which bodes poorly for performance of poor readers in regular classrooms.

Armed with your predictions, a list of measures that you think you want to collect, and your indomitable spirit, you are ready. All you need to do is find schools with different programs, collect the data about what they do, and compare the outcome variables.

Having selected a research project to conduct in a school setting, you are ready for the remainder of this book. In it we attempt to describe the ins and outs of school research. We describe many of the practical pitfalls that occur in educational settings, drawing on our experiences and those of our colleagues to address the major issues that typically emerge in school-based research endeavors. Topics covered include selecting schools and building relationships with them; developing an understanding of the perspectives of the school personnel and how research projects might be viewed as collaborative projects that serve the interests of both groups; specific issues in working with teachers and other school personnel; practical issues related to selection of measures; difficulties in and issues surrounding the development of longitudinal data sets; how to prepare to deal with opportunities that can emerge; and what to consider when things go wrong, as they inevitably will. Throughout the book, we attempt to tie in research methods issues (like design, sampling, informed consent, measurement, and timing). Finally, we assume that somehow you get through it all and actually collect your data; at that point your work becomes analyses, inferences, and communicating to the audiences with a potential interest in what you found.

We take you through these topics both by a general discussion of the issues but also by applications and illustrations. In many instances, we will use for our illustrations the example introduced in this chapter, a study asking whether the children called "slow learners," "low achieving," or "learning disabled" perform better in regular classrooms or in special education, "pullout" programs. We also present additional illustrations that exemplify other types of studies and different designs. Most important for persons interested in beginning to work in schools, we attempt to provide a better understanding of the culture of schools and of the types of practical problems that can be anticipated.

EXERCISES

NOTE: Please remember our suggestion that you think about the issues individually, then discuss them in small groups, and finally share your ideas with the whole class. Appoint a recorder to keep track of your group's ideas so you can present them to other class members.

2. *Recollections of School Research.* Try to recall any research done in classes where you were a student. We expect that few if any readers will remember research done in their schools, but if you do, how many of the following questions can you answer: What was done? Who did it? What were the purposes? Were there any incentives for participation? What feedback did you get about the research? Do you remember whether/how your teacher introduced the research and the teacher's views about the research—nonverbal as well as verbal cues? Consider what if any feedback you received. Did you receive anything valuable in return for your participation? If you cannot remember any research, can you think of teaching techniques or class materials that you particularly enjoyed or disliked? Try to use them to generate a research question.

3. *Achievement of Low-Achieving Children.* The issue to consider here is whether low-achieving children would do better in regular classrooms or in separate classrooms. Which of the competing views presented in this chapter seems most reasonable to you? For which dimensions (e.g., grades, standardized tests, social skills, happiness) and why? Practice generating hypotheses (i.e., predictions) related to this issue and justifying them. Feel free to speculate, for at this point the process of idea generation and hypothesis formulation is more important than the accuracy of the ideas. Save your hypotheses to use for Exercise 7.

2

Getting Started:
Accessing School Populations

In this chapter, we assume that readers have chosen a problem and are attempting to find a setting in which to conduct their research. As noted previously, there are different reasons to work in educational settings and different goals and objectives that might be sought. To return to the distinction drawn by Cronbach and Suppes (1969) between decision-oriented and conclusion-oriented research (discussed in Chapter 1), we assume that the impetus for research comes from the researcher, namely, that you are conducting conclusion-oriented research. If your work could interest educators as well as yourself, your life should be simplified: Their interest will facilitate your progress in addressing the issues raised in this chapter. There are few things more valuable to educational researchers than a school staff interested in and committed to the research project.

This chapter is focused less on instances in which schools or funding agencies identify a practical problem and seek researchers to work on it (i.e., they lead researchers to conduct decision-oriented research), which is not to say that such research is uncommon or less important. In fact, much of the current interest in schools occurs because of the "education crisis"—the perception that schools are experiencing major problems that demand immediate attention. Further, solutions seem likely to come from research dedicated to solving those problems. As a consequence, the research community has been under pressure to work collaboratively with school staff, parents, and communities to address problems. If researchers fail to work collaboratively with educators and parents, they are seen as elitist and unconcerned with the issues of the people who actually are affected by their research. Thus, educational researchers today are likely to be involved in cooperative ventures that address practical problems.

If the impetus for decision-oriented research comes from a funding agency, researchers likely still will have to identify sites in which to conduct the research, and the circumstances will be very similar to those of researcher-initiated studies we describe in this chapter. If, however, the schools seek investigators to help them with their problems, issues of access will be very different and should be greatly simplified. Difficulties can still emerge, in particular, internal conflict between central administrators and school administrators, between school administrators and teachers, or among teachers within a building. In other words, whenever commitment of the school staff who will be involved in the project is questionable, the importance of the issues raised in this chapter increases.

GENERAL ISSUES IN FINDING A RESEARCH SITE

We decided in Chapter 1 that we are going to do school-based research. Our next step is to find a school or schools in which to conduct that research. Even though this seems like an easy and straightforward task, it typically is not. First, we need to find out what is already going on in those schools in which we might want to work, and we need to know about obstacles that might preclude certain schools or districts from being available. Many of the obstacles are practical ones. For example, school districts closest to universities and colleges typically get frequent requests to participate in research. School personnel may eventually be overwhelmed by requests from eager folks like us and lose interest or develop resistance to additional overtures.

Even if we find no resistance to participating in research, we still have the basic problem of where to start. For example, whom do we contact? How about people who design the curriculum. But at what level? District, building, grade, class? Well, if that choice seems confusing, maybe we could just go to the main administrators and ask them. But we run into the same problem: district level (superintendent) or building level (principal). Could we just go to specific classrooms?

In fact, selecting sites for research is one of those problems that seems never to get easier no matter how much experience you obtain. You can start almost anywhere, with anyone, and still by chance and blind luck end up right where you want to be. Or you can do everything correctly, use all the proper techniques and approaches, and still end up stymied and frustrated. The people in some school districts, whether because of their culture, poor morale, or other factors seem totally uninterested in research regardless of what they have you believe initially or how they lead you on.

Our experience has shown that it is possible to start at any level and with a wide range of contact persons and still gain entry to schools. In part, the type of research that you want to do may determine where you start. If you want to work with only one or two classes, a reasonable starting point may be contacting one or a few teachers. If you want to work with entire schools, contacting a principal may be more appropriate, as the principal is likely to be the only person with the authority to commit an entire school staff to a research project. If you want to work in several schools within a single district, you should begin by seeking permission from a district-level administrator who can act as an advocate for you in more than one school or at least provide you with legitimate access.

Regardless of your starting point, the typical permission process ultimately involves the same individuals. Approval will require review at the building level and at the district level. Administrators today are unlikely to approve a research project without giving teachers a say (which of course is not necessarily the same as getting them enthusiastic about the project), so teachers, principals, and other administrators usually will become involved. Unfortunately, regardless of your starting point, much of your success in gaining access to schools may depend upon factors over which you have little if any control. For example, is someone within the schools willing to be an open and forceful advocate of your project—the type of advocate described by Wahlstrom (1990): "Well, she was just very assertive and very strong in her opinions. I mean, she does not back down from what she believes in. She is very forceful about trying to get that information to you" (p. 260). At the same time, it will be important for you to watch how strong advocates are perceived by other school staff. If they are seen as status-seeking loudmouths by most others, your proposal could be dead in the water before you begin.

One way to help researchers to think about the roles of various contact persons is to ask persons working in schools how they think ideas get spread and how changes have been made in their schools. Wahlstrom's (1990) study provides illustrative comments from teachers and administrators about school decision making. The teachers recognized they needed to work through their principal; as one stated, "You definitely go through steps. . . . We go to the principal first" (p. 138). A teacher from a different district said, "I'm sure that if he hadn't agreed with this idea, that it never would have gotten off the ground . . . and I wouldn't have known where else to go" (p. 263). And from another: "If it doesn't go past [the principal] then it's not going to go anywhere" (p. 138). Would they go directly to the school board? "It would not be acceptable" (p. 138), and "I would never do that, and I can't imagine anyone here on staff doing it" (p. 138). Administrators may in some instances bypass teachers; for example, "In the whole administrative decision, we were not [involved]" (p. 220). Higher-level administrators also recognized the critical role of the principal; as stated by a curriculum director, "Principals can keep things off agendas for staff meetings" (p. 262). The principals recognized their gatekeeping functions. One said about any idea brought to the school by a teacher, "You know, I can pretty much kill it or sidetrack it at that point" (p. 137). Another principal expressed his feelings about teachers attempting to bypass him, "I'd kill a person if they go around and go up the ladder . . . that's not fair. . . . [The teachers] know how I operate and they'll get a fair hearing" (pp. 138-139).

To avoid leaving the impression that administrators ignore or disregard their teachers' views, we conclude with a remark by a superintendent, "In terms of major reform, unless I have absolute consensus of representative teachers, I won't move. This is because it's not going to work unless they're interested in it, so I ultimately will decide to not [approve of a reform] unless I have a consensus" (p. 285). The comment clearly evidences a consultative processes—but also the fact that the superintendent will ultimately decide.

As we discuss school changes, it is important to keep in mind that the school staff may not be thinking about the same things we researchers are when we talk about innovation or change. School districts are always more interested in research on problems they define rather than on those researchers define, so the comments quoted above may be presuming a greater interest on the speakers' part than you may experience in your project. Indeed, if the research project is initiated by the researcher without involvement of school staff, the primary problem may be getting anyone at the school interested in and willing to support the project rather than in selecting the ideal person to have involved in the research.

In addition, school problems are typically practical rather than theoretical, and what school staff think of as research may frequently be viewed by academics as simply evaluation of a minor permutation of existing procedures or techniques rather than as conceptually important or interesting research. The point here is not to demean practical work as irrelevant, for the "action research" tradition (see Lewin, 1946) clearly established how theory could guide research and be tested while addressing important practical problems. Further, there is value in examining the generalizability of phenomena to various educational settings. It seems likely, however, that the point of diminishing return for research is reached before the practical issues are all resolved, and what might seem to be important issues to educators may be already widely understood and viewed as mundane by the research community. The important point to keep in mind is that it is worthwhile to make sure that from the beginning there is agreement about what is to be accomplished as well as the roles of various participants in attempting to accomplish the goals.

IDENTIFYING RESEARCH SITES
AND CONTACT PERSONS

How will you go about identifying schools and districts that may have the kinds of programs that are of interest to you? As a starting point, you could find knowledgeable individuals at your college or university. A good source of information about programs would be faculty in colleges of education with student teachers and their own research projects in schools. In addition, education majors currently placed as student teachers can describe in detail what goes on in the classes in which they work.

A second way of getting information would be contacting persons at state or regional departments of education, who most likely have initiatives such as model programs, demonstration projects, and other innovations being conducted in schools. They might be able to match you up with schools attempting to develop programs consistent with your research interests. They also may have lists of schools with specific types of educational programs.

Third, you could read current or recent newspapers, looking for articles about specific schools developing strategies or programs of interest to you. If you fail to find relevant articles, you might call the education reporter(s) for your city newspaper to find out what schools are doing interesting things. As an important aside, note that a risk in trying to work with "outstanding" schools is that they have little to gain and much to lose in their reputation if research shows them to be ineffective. In addition, if they really are outstanding, they are likely to be innovative and to have a number of projects already ongoing. Thus, they may be unenthusiastic about your ideas because they are too busy or already have research projects in progress. Schools with no research tradition or with identified problems might be more interested, receptive, and creative, for they have clear needs to be met and fewer alternative distractions.

A fourth alternative would be contacting curriculum specialists at the school district or the building level. If the school district is large, such individuals are likely to have broad responsibilities and therefore not be familiar with particular details. They may, however, be able to direct you to someone closer to specific programs.

Many studies conducted in schools start in ways much different from those described above. They can start from informal contacts and the discovery of common interests and ideas between researchers and other individuals, such as teachers who are interested in developing specific types of programs to use in their classes; from education students who are also practicing teachers and who want to try out the new ideas that they are learning in their own classes; from parents who are interested in promoting certain types of educational programs; and even from school districts experiencing problems who come to the "experts" at the universities for help.

One final way in which research begins is from the availability of research funds. Federal and state funding priorities channel research in specific directions and encourage school districts and educational researchers to form partnerships to work in the areas desired. Closely linked to funding priorities is political redirection in education; when agencies move schools toward particular orientations or approaches (e.g., outcome-based education, site-based management, assurance of mastery), then resources need to be funneled in those directions and plans need to be made on how to accomplish the desired changes effectively. During political redirection there is great opportunity for researchers to receive access in exchange for their advice and training.

Unfortunately, researchers new to educational settings lack entry to many of the above means of access, which limits their opportunities. Furthermore, new researchers may ignore the fact that many school staff members feel overworked and have little reason to welcome disruptions caused by researchers. In the beginning you may have to settle for less than you want and spend time building up your credibility with school personnel before gaining access for larger projects.

Our recent project with students who had mild disabilities illustrates a number of approaches that can work and a couple that didn't. We started with identifying three school districts that were each attempting to implement a distinct theory-driven mainstream integration program to serve students with mild disabilities. Such children have special needs, but can participate during most of the school day in the regular classroom. Although they are labeled learning disabled or mildly mentally handicapped, their common defining characteristic is that typically they are the lowest-achieving students in their classrooms. Each of the districts was using a different intervention, so a three-treatment-condition design seemed appropriate for our research. Further, two of the districts were using strategies that faculty from the University of Minnesota were instrumental in developing, so they already had consulted with us and our colleagues. In other words, relationships already had been established and the perception of mutual gain had been developed.

Our original plan was to select three schools from each of three districts and find comparison schools for each of the three types of programs. Each comparison school would need to be serving low-achieving students in resource programs that pulled children out of the regular classrooms and served them in special programs for basic skill remediation. The situation was complicated by the fact that all three mainstreaming school districts had been involved for the past two or three years in a state-led school effectiveness project designed to improve schools by focusing on topics known to be related to school effectiveness. There was the possibility that this state project could have been greatly improving the effectiveness of the participating schools independently of any mainstreaming programs that they were using.

As is probably true of most unwanted complexities in educational settings, the complication had mixed effects upon our work. Even though the school effectiveness project complicated our lives by forcing us to attempt to find comparison schools that were also participating in that project, it also helped us to find comparison schools by providing us with general information about what was going on in a number of schools. More important, it gave us a link to and identified contact persons at the state department of education; those persons had a listing of participating schools and were somewhat interested in our project. Thus, they were willing to write a letter of encouragement and support that accompanied our initial contacts with schools.

In our attempts to select as comparison schools ones that had participated in the school effectiveness project for two or three years, we contacted a number of schools to obtain specific details about the kinds of programs that they had in place and any changes they were planning. Our initial search for comparison schools included 22 schools. We chose in the first year of our project to assess school climate in all of those schools as well as our nine target schools. As measures of climate, we focused on 15 characteristics of effective schools that the state school effectiveness project had identified and that formed the basis for school improvement efforts. (For a description of these characteristics, see Maruyama, Deno, Cohen, & Espin, 1989.) In short, we were able to find three schools that served students with mild disabilities in pullout programs (i.e., special classes outside the regular classroom) and that were reasonably well matched demographically and by climate measures. We should note, however, that our success was likely due in no small part to our being able to offer each participating school $3,500 per year to support staff development efforts; to put the amount into context, it represented five times the money typically available to the schools.

Lest readers think that all went smoothly, we will briefly describe some of the obstacles that we encountered. One of the three mainstreaming districts withdrew from our study just as we began, leaving us three schools short. The schools had been part of a multidistrict educational cooperative formed to serve special education students, and just as our project began, the cooperative was reconfigured and those particular schools left for another cooperative. Because our contact was the special education director of the cooperative, the schools withdrew from our project also. Obviously, there is more to educational research than just having incentives. We were forced to take as replacements schools from three different districts, including two schools that were only beginning to implement the intervention and one that hadn't been involved in the school effectiveness project.

Before succumbing to the temptation to conclude that such a chain of events was exceptional, consider the experiences of two other projects that addressed similar research questions. Both received federal funds to examine what could be accomplished for low-achieving students by incorporating "all that was known" about enhancing mainstream classrooms to support low-achieving students. In one instance, after receiving the grant award, the researchers had to find a different school to work in because, despite prior approval from the principal and district administrators, the teachers refused to participate. In the second instance, after five months of working with the school, the researchers felt compelled to look for a different school because the principal and staff could not organize themselves to incorporate effectively the intervention strategies required for supporting low-achieving students. We encountered additional difficulties in getting our interventions going. The staff development plans were implemented more slowly than we would have liked and were less focused on issues relevant to the project than had been our hope. Assessing the impact of the interventions was immensely complicated by different schools developing variants of the interventions and implementing them at different rates. Although such a situation may be viewed as a great opportunity by persons who relish analyzing their data with exotic quasi-experimental designs, results defying easy interpretation are also guaranteed. (For further discussion of designs, see Chapter 4; see also Campbell & Stanley, 1963; Cook & Campbell, 1979.)

Staff turnover also caused unexpected problems. In one school the principal changed from the first year to the second, resulting in a new person implementing the intervention and maintaining contacts with us. In another school, the district superintendent resigned between years 1 and 2 of our project, and our project was administered by an interim superintendent during the second and third years.

Finally, we should note that our primary contact persons varied from site to site. In one district, we worked primarily with a district consultant who was a self-employed "grantsman" rather than with a full-time employee of the district. That situation ultimately worked satisfactorily, but produced some strange moments, because the consultant was not a staff member of the district, but in many ways an outsider like us. Working with consultants is not an approach we recommend, for other research suggests it is a very difficult one to make work effectively and requires a highly skilled consultant who is expert in the approach chosen and in staff development (see McLaughlin, 1990).

In the other district that had three schools participating in our study, we worked with the superintendent. In that district commitment to the project was no problem, but working though the superintendent removed us a step from the buildings and from directly shaping what went on in them (recall the earlier remark by a superintendent about the importance of teacher participation). As noted above, in the district that dropped out of our study, we had been working with the special education director from a multidistrict educational cooperative. That arrangement was also somewhat unusual, both because such a person is likely found only in small rural districts and also because the special education director of such a cooperative typically has less direct influence within the administration of the local school districts. In the remaining six schools we initially made contacts with the principals. We found having the leader of the building involved in the project a good arrangement for implementing building-level changes. Success then depends heavily on the commitment of the principal and the principal's capacity to engage the school staff. If that commitment is made, however, direct influence on programs is possible. Incidentally, we anticipate that because of increased emphasis in school reform efforts on building-level autonomy in governance and budgets through "site-based management," much future research necessarily will require working closely with individual principals and school staff.

Perhaps some readers might wonder why, after we earlier spoke of contact persons potentially coming from all levels, in no instance did our contacts start at the level of the classroom teacher. Given the tight time lines we were working under (i.e., one year to get going), we chose the most efficient route given the current shift toward site-based management—that is, we worked with the building supervisor, the principal. Although it is also possible to begin at the teacher level, for interventions like ours that operate at the building level and need participation from all classes, that approach is more complicated. It is difficult to get implementation at that level filtering upward from individual teachers. Further, regardless of the source of the initiative, the principal needs to approve and often can kill initiatives if he or she is skeptical or uninterested (recall the comments by teachers and other school personnel). Classroom-level research can much more readily begin at the teacher level, however.

OBTAINING CONSENT FROM PARTICIPANTS

We assume at this point that you have persisted and been rewarded in your efforts by gaining access to schools. Now it is time to gain formal approval to use human subjects in research. Not only do you have to worry about your school's guidelines about research subjects, which typically are enforced by an institutional review board (see Sieber, 1992), you also need to find out about the school district's regulations. Regulations can vary greatly from district to district, depending often on past experience with research and sometimes reflecting reactions to unpleasant experiences. Some districts deny access to file information, or at least to information on subjects like race demographics or test score performance, whereas others allow only indirect access (e.g., a school staff member has to gather it for you and, in many instances, remove identifying information to protect anonymity of students). Still other districts or schools may open their files for you provided you promise to maintain confidentiality and to preserve individual anonymity. (We will return to this topic in more detail in a later chapter.) Regardless of the particulars, having to determine and adapt to the policies and practices of your particular schools is another reminder that you have entered a different culture with its own set of rules.

BUILDING PRELIMINARY RELATIONSHIPS

Now that you've gained access to schools and untangled the regulations about the use of human subjects for research, you are almost ready to get going. There remain some other preliminaries. Ideally, you should familiarize yourself with the school culture and personnel. That would include taking time to observe ongoing school processes and talking to staff and students. A necessary effort is to schedule a meeting with staff members who will be involved in the project. You need to explain the project to them and solicit their reactions to it. At this stage, anything you can do to increase their stake in the project is a major plus. Do not underestimate the importance of their feeling a sense of ownership. For example, altering your project time line to accommodate their concerns over class time, scheduling, and so forth can be a small price to pay for enthusiastic cooperation. Adding measures of interest to them may be possible even if the measures don't address the conceptual issues that you think are central. (As an aside, it is probably worthwhile at this point generally to agree on the full array of measures; some districts may at this point even ask you not to add any further measures or requirements later in the project. It is probably a good idea to attempt to keep the school staff as flexible on this topic as possible.) Providing backup staffing to compensate for time school staff commits to the research project can be a valuable way to create goodwill (see Cohen, 1990). Adding replacement teachers to implement the intervention if your study involves instructional interventions is a reasonable way to assure uniformity of the treatments as well as to provide teachers a small reward for participating. (They can view the replacement teacher as someone to give them a break or as someone who can train them in new techniques.)

In the project we have been using to illustrate how various techniques can work, we had too many participating schools that were too widely scattered geographically to spend much time in each one. As an attempt to compensate for not having spent much time in each school, we designated a staff person, typically a regular classroom teacher, to be our liaison at that school. That person was called the building-level project coordinator. For fairly nominal compensation, our building-level coordinators assisted us by distributing the instruments to be filled out by school staff, collecting those instruments after they were completed, adding codes to assure anonymity of respondents, and finally, sending the instruments back to us. The coordinators also helped us to schedule times for data collection from students.

The presence of building-level coordinators allowed us to have our data distributed and picked up by persons who were friends of and familiar with the respondents. The approach worked very well; we had virtually no problems with nonresponse. Once again a subtle difference, in this instance the question of who has contact with the respondents, had an apparent impact on how the respondents viewed the project and their timeliness in responding.

The above discussion should not be viewed as suggesting that we could or wanted to avoid altogether meeting with school staff. We met with staff to explain the nature of the intervention and to give staff the opportunity to ask questions about the intervention. In addition, we met with them to provide staff development training related to the interventions. Finally, our staff went out to the schools to collect the data from children.

In summary, in this chapter we discussed the concerns and issues of getting research in schools started. The discussion included (a) suggestions about how to find schools that are doing things that may interest researchers, (b) some implications of starting by contacting various school personnel, and (c) illustrations drawn from our recent experiences. Finally, we noted the necessity of gaining an understanding of school policies about data access and using human subjects, and discussed the kinds of activities that are necessary to gain staff acceptance of and commitment to the project.

EXERCISES

4. *Contacts for Different Types of Research Questions.* Try to identify three different types of research questions that might require initial contact at the three different levels (i.e., teacher, principal, and district). What would be reasons for initiating contact at each of the three levels and what might the risks be of starting in the wrong place?

5. *Teachers and Research.* Contact a regular classroom teacher and talk to that person about: (a) whether research is being done in his or her school, (b) how the research approval process works in that school, and (c) how staff members feel about participating in research projects.

3

Establishing Credibility, Increasing Understanding, and Gaining Commitment: Dreaming an Impossible Dream?

At this point, we assume that you have identified schools that are interested in your project and you have begun to talk to the school staff about specifics. You have spent a little time in the school sites and are beginning to get a sense of how these schools operate. Incidentally, you may find as you begin to look carefully at schools and what goes on in them, that you are surprised by the broad array of different *interesting* research projects that could be done in schools. There are a number of important practical problems that can be addressed at the same time as you attempt to answer important conceptual questions.

The possibilities for theoretically interesting and practically important findings within a single project is a major draw of applied research generally and educational research in particular; unlike the situation with some types of basic research, the relevance to real problems of research conducted in authentic settings is immediately apparent. When researchers talk about research conducted in authentic settings as being high in external validity, they mean that the findings are intended to be applied to settings virtually identical to the ones in which the research was conducted, and therefore, those findings should be applicable in a fairly direct, straightforward fashion.

Having described a major lure of research conducted in educational settings, we must place that lure in perspective. One tendency we have noticed in some inexperienced researchers as they plan research in applied settings like schools is the tendency for them to try to accomplish too much too soon and to expand what they initially had planned to do. Once you see the range of possible problems that could be addressed, there is the temptation to extend your study or to try to get more than one study going at the same time. Our advice is to start simply, to stay focused despite distractions, and to save the new ideas

for future times and projects. Avoid behaving like a kid in a candy store
and focus on the project that you have planned. It will likely require
more effort than you expect.

This chapter covers a number of aspects that will take time, including
preparation, planning, and coordination. Most important, we here adopt
a perspective that examines the orientations of the different individuals
who have an investment in what happens in schools. First, we will look
at some potential consequences resulting from the types of perspectives
that are brought to schools by researchers; second, we discuss the
interplay of needs of researchers with needs of teachers and students; and
third, we describe some ways of establishing equitable relationships.
Finally, in conclusion, we begin to discuss how to develop realistic time
lines for getting work done.

THE PERSPECTIVES OF RESEARCHERS
AND EDUCATORS

Researcher and Other Outsider Perspectives

Exercise 1 at the end of the Preface asked you to think about the
images of schools that affect the ways you think about schools, and
Exercise 2 at the end of Chapter 1 asked you to try to recall any
educational research that was done in your classes when you were a
student. Those recollections are important, for they help remind us that
our ideas about schools and what goes on in them are strongly influenced by our experiences when we were students. As researchers, we
bring into schools images from our past, both about how schools are
and about what they should be in order to be effective. Unlike many
other settings with which we have only indirect contacts (e.g., even
though most of us learn how federal and state governments operate, we
likely have little firsthand experience with them), schools are institutions with which we each have had firsthand, direct contacts over an
extended period of time. The nature of the contacts and their consequences vary, but most people feel that they have some good ideas if
not some expertise about what works in schools and what does not work.

Perhaps reflecting the diverse array of experiences and recollections
that individuals have about schools, there is little convergence of
opinions about what works in schools. Although problematic for making policy decisions, divergent views are probably good for science and

theory; these differences increase the likelihood that a body of diverse research will be generated, but at the same time, make it difficult for policymakers to choose from among the different approaches. What are the implications for researchers of differing beliefs regarding educational approaches? School staff members' preferences shape the strategies they advocate or use. Their preferences are tempered, however, by structural limitations; few schools will attempt to accommodate a broad range of instructional techniques or adapt instruction to every individual difference in learning style.

The effects of researchers' preferences seem to be somewhat more subtle. Beliefs about what schools are like and about what works in them act as a filter through which researchers view schools and through which they evaluate research programs. For example, even if all researchers accepted and believed in research arguing for the effectiveness of cooperative learning approaches, differences in other beliefs, such as the extent to which children should depend upon others for their learning, or about how fair and equitable it is to assign group grades, might determine whether such techniques are tried. In addition, differences in beliefs about the value of competition may dictate whether cooperative approaches are examined as well as whether the approaches chosen include interteam competitions to complement intrateam cooperative learning interventions.

Overall, then, as researchers we need to be aware of our biases and preconceptions and attempt to move beyond thinking, "After all, I went to school once, and that's where I learned most of what I know, and I remember what worked [i.e., what I liked] and what didn't work [i.e., what I'd change], so . . . " In contrast to such thinking, we have to accept that as we return to these "lands of our youth" we are the foreigners who need to learn about the environments in which we want to work. We come to those settings as adult researchers rather than as former students, and our understandings of schools can be enriched by individuals with other experiences in them.

Learning About School Perspectives

As noted earlier, schools each have their own culture. Understanding that culture requires both careful observation and finding individuals who will provide honest answers to any questions you might want to ask. Unfortunately, gaining an understanding of the less apparent dynamics of the culture typically requires your being accepted into that culture. If you are seen as a part of the culture, you may find yourself privy to inside information that is shared informally. If you are allowed to be present during informal conversations among school staff, particularly outside of work settings, you may obtain a much better understanding of what actually goes on than you ever could from observing behaviors. As an illustration of the importance of the culture of the school, imagine, for example, that you want to implement an approach that has been used successfully in a number of school settings. Even if the approach has been wildly successful elsewhere, you need to explore how it will fit into the school setting in which you want to work. Concerning research design, you may well run into circumstances where you have to make a choice between fidelity of treatment and compatibility of treatment with the school curriculum (more on this later). Careful selection of school sites could potentially avoid this situation, but changes in school programs may produce the problem no matter how carefully you plan.

Our focus on the importance of understanding the context and climate of particular schools may seem excessive, but it reflects the outcome of our own and our colleagues' experiences. Rule 1 is to do as much as you can to understand the environment in which you will be working. We have found, for example, that conducting in-service workshops for staff gives us important clues about how staff members interact, about the nature of the relationship between the principal and the teachers, about staff members' willingness to embrace change and to attempt to improve what they do, and about their openness to outsiders. Even if you lack such opportunities (in our case example, the opportunities came from trading our skills in providing staff development for access), you need to find ways of involving yourself in the school. Sitting in on staff meetings or assisting teachers for a short period of time or making a presentation to students as an outside expert may give you insights that will help you design research studies. Some schools may be reluctant to let outsiders become involved even as observers; earlier we noted that one possible type of collaboration involves teachers who are also students and are open to ideas that improve their teaching—if possible, researchers should develop contacts with persons inside the school, who know and understand its ways and will act as an advocate for the research.

Of course, there are alternative means of learning about the schools in which you want to work. One that more closely follows a traditional research program would be running a pilot study that gets you involved with staff in the culture of the schools. Pilot studies can be very helpful, particularly if you get feedback from staff about how the study actually worked in the classes, what really happened, and how it can be improved.

One of our experiences in pilot tests of our data collection procedures with a sample of first graders illustrates both how much can be learned from such testing and how the culture of schools can operate. As our research assistants administered our instruments, they realized that the measures were too difficult for 6- and 7-year-olds. Imagine our anxiety over giving the students tasks that they can't do! Fortunately, we were saved when the principal interrupted our pilot efforts by announcing over the PA system that it was time to celebrate Martin Luther King, Jr., Day. The teachers, students, and our staff immediately stopped the pilot testing, went out into the halls, joined hands, and, fittingly, sang "We Shall Overcome."

In some circumstances it may be unwise to conduct a pilot study in the same setting that you plan to use. Situations in which pilot testing might well be unwise include (a) using an approach that is new and potentially exciting and risks diffusion of treatment (i.e., other teachers who are not in the treatment conditions informally adopting aspects of the treatment to use in their classes) or major changes occurring in school practices (e.g., the entire school adopting the method); (b) the subject population is so small that you cannot afford to lose the test subjects you will be unable to use again in the larger study; or (c) you require substantial class time for the intervention. Some of these circumstances may only warrant working in a different setting, but others might bring more broadly into question the issue of pilot testing. In any event, you should look for alternative ways of learning about the schools in which you want to do research.

To summarize, we suggest that researchers initially attempt to examine and understand the perspective they bring to schools (What do you remember about schools? Where do those recollections come from? How do they affect your thinking about educational research?). Link your perspective to the approaches you choose and to what actually is going on at the school sites you are likely to use in the research. Linkages with schools can be built through observation, through a pilot study, or through involving school staff in your project.

MEETING THE NEEDS OF BOTH
RESEARCHERS AND EDUCATORS

For researchers, a mark of venturing into a new project is enthusiasm coupled with energy. But what if in your interactions with school staff you sense no great enthusiasm among most of them either for your ideas or for your commitment to doing educational research. Is it them? Are they just punching the clock until retirement? Should you consider giving up on this site, or on the idea altogether? Maybe you are being too quick to judge them. Maybe the fact that they have been around longer than you have means something. Maybe their perspective on research in schools derives from the lackluster history of research in schools that has attempted to improve education. Maybe we're naive, idealistic, and overenthusiastic, and they're reasonable and pragmatic?

There may also be some middle ground to explore before adopting extreme interpretations. You might try to gain a meeting of the minds that couples your eagerness with their savvy and experience. You might ask them what they think could be modified and what would increase their enthusiasm. Focus on constructive comments from teachers who seem to understand what you want to do. We suggest a number of areas to probe:

1. Do they really understand what you are trying to accomplish? If not, how can you explain what you are doing in a way that will be understood?

If they do understand and still seem uninterested, it's time for probing a second area:

2. What reservations do they have about what you are trying to accomplish? Is it likely from their perspective your research will have no effect or waste their time? Is it too esoteric? Are there links missing between the conceptualizing and the operationalizing? Is your research inconsistent with what they have learned? Are there alternative ways to set up the study that might make them feel more comfortable?

If staff members both understand and accept the premises underlying your work, perhaps there are problems linked to their work, which is the next area to probe:

3. Are you asking them to do too much? Does the study lack potential benefits for either teachers or students? Does it take up a lot of class time? Remember that for some teachers, virtually any activity that requires them to do something different from what they are currently doing will be perceived as increasing their work load and will therefore be viewed unfavorably.

Think of these questions as an opportunity for teachers to tell you what they think and for you to try to better understand their perspective. The specific questions are intended as providing a generic set of suggestions; the actual questions you ask will depend upon the nature of your study and what you need to know. Other questions may emerge from your initial interviews with teachers and other school staff.

Up to this point, we have suggested that you assume that staff members are well intentioned and the issues they raise are legitimate ones that really concern them. Unfortunately, however, there also may be situations in which the goal of at least some of the school staff is to disrupt your work and to delay you as long as possible, for example, if they just don't want to be bothered with anything extra. In such instances it may be very difficult to get at the underlying reasons, for, as with many academic arguments, those reasons get cloaked in reasonable-sounding rhetoric. Only experience and inside contacts can help you to sort real arguments from specious ones. Fortunately, in most instances there are few sanctions against criticizing researchers, so staff members are likely to be blunt. Exceptions are more likely to come when school leaders are backing your research or when opposition to your work may be viewed as reflecting unfavored beliefs, such as ones tied to racism or prejudice.

One means of cementing relations with educators is to be concrete. If teachers have a role in your work, spell it out to them as clearly as possible. When in doubt, include more detail than you think they need, for you want to be sure that the instructions are understood. That does not mean that teachers will do what you want them to do, but it does assure that if they want to help you, they have the information they need. To the extent that you provide materials that can lead them and the students through the exercises or activities, you are imposing less work on them and increasing the likelihood that the intervention will be implemented as intended.

As early as possible, provide school staff with a time line of when things need to be done, when class time is needed, when surveys need to be completed and returned, and so forth. Reassure the staff that you will not be dropping surprises on them at your whim and fancy, and give them enough lead time to fit your activities into their routine. Provide a list of specific tasks that need to be accomplished and when they need to be done. As an example, Table 3.1 provides the time line we used with 12 schools in our case example. We described the events that would occur as part of our project, when those events would occur, who the events would involve, and where appropriate, who would be responsible for collecting information.

In addition, it is important to give staff members feedback and let them know the outcomes. As much as possible, tell them when you will be completing your analyses and presenting preliminary findings for discussion. Schedule a meeting at a time that is convenient for school staff. Even if no one attends the meeting, you have given participants the opportunity to see what happens after the data collection part of the study finishes. Other ways of providing feedback and information to include in the feedback will be covered in more detail in a later chapter.

To summarize, in this section we have suggested ways of giving staff opportunities to provide you with feedback. Such feedback might not be used, but it should be seen as an additional opportunity to see how practitioners think about your ideas and what obstacles you might encounter. You might even discover ways of improving your study, which would make the additional effort worthwhile. Finally, we have provided concrete examples of ways of implicitly suggesting to school staff that you respect what goes on in the schools, that you consider the staff members to be participants in the research, and that you are trying to understand their perspectives on your work as well as your own.

SCHOOL RESEARCH AS AN
EXCHANGE RELATIONSHIP

Perhaps the hardest thing for neophyte educational researchers to learn is that their work is not likely to be inherently and intrinsically interesting to most educators. Thus, even though we made the point previously, we return to it here in the context of exchange relationships.

Table 3.1
LD/MH Research Project Event Chart, Year 2

Dates	Events/Areas of Concern	Instruments	Data Collector	Participants
Sept. 1988	Implementation of staff development activities			
Oct. 1988 April 1989	Identification of lowest-achieving students in reading in each classroom	BASS	Teachers	Entire class
Oct. 1988 April 1989	Students' attitudes about school	School Attitude Survey	Teachers	Entire class
Nov. 1988	Collection of IEPs for LD and MH students who receive services in reading	IEPs in reading	School staff	
Dec. 1988	Description of reading programs received by LD, MH, and low-achieving students	Program description	Teachers	Teachers
Jan. 1989	Collection of background information on IEP'd and low-achieving students	Information sheets	School staff	School staff
Feb. 1989	Staff perceptions of school characteristics	School Characteristics Survey	BLC	School staff
Feb. 1989	Topical marker (i.e., attention, memory)	Phonemic representation	LD/MH staff	LD/MH/LA students
Feb. 1989	Student ability	Otis-Lennon	LD/MH staff	LD/MH/LA students
Feb. 1989	Academic self-concept	Self-Perception Profile for LD students	LD/MH Staff	LD/MH/LA students
Feb. 1989	Student's behavioral and emotional adjustment	Rating scale	Teachers	Teachers

Key to abbreviations: BASS = Basic Academic Skills Samples; IEP = Individualized Educational Plan; LD = Learning Disabled; MH = Mildly Handicapped; BLC = Building-Level Coordinator; LA = Low Achieving

One way to view school-based research is as an exchange between the research community and the teaching community. Quite frankly, even though we might wish for a situation in which teachers as a part of their training were given the expectation that participating in school improvement research is a common and necessary part of being a teacher, and thus participating in research required no extrinsic motivators, this usually is not the case. Most teachers never develop the expectation that their job requires them to participate in school improvement research because they have little exposure to ongoing school research projects. Thus, they never gain an appreciation for the important interplay between research and practice.

In other words, it is probably reasonable to enter into the research experience with the expectation that it will be an exchange relationship. Researchers obtain access to research subjects by providing things like staff development training (including teacher license renewal or academic credits), discretionary time for teachers, and, possibly, small rewards for student participants. Finally, if you can help the teachers solve their problems, they are more likely to be interested in helping you with yours.

Even though mutual needs seem to provide a likely avenue for establishing good working relationships between researchers and educators, such needs don't guarantee that the relationships will develop. Some school district staff members purposefully or otherwise send out a strong message that they really are not interested in research being done in their schools. Consider, for example, the circumstances encountered by one of our colleagues, who has been working to develop a program of strategies for improving the reading abilities of early elementary grade children who have difficulty learning to read. For a two-year period, she worked with several school districts in implementing the program and found strong empirical support for her program. Then during the fall of 1990, a major Minnesota urban school district failed in its attempt to pass a school tax levy to implement a costly but generally effective program for providing remedial instruction in reading (called Reading Recovery). Because the levy failed, one would think that the district would search eagerly for an alternative program that would not be costly to implement, that is, programs that could be bootstrapped for the short term. Our colleague lined up research support for training school staff and then implementing her approach in several schools. Then she contacted the district director of elementary education. That person took a month (and several more calls and messages) to respond, and four months later had only assigned a staff person to follow up the initial inquiry with our colleague. At least implicitly, that district seems to have expressed a positive disinclination for the project. Unless you can tolerate such frustrations and are willing to endure similar frustrations throughout a project, accepting failure is a reasonable decision. Barring overriding interest in that district, it seems more sensible to acknowledge a refusal and inquire elsewhere. Ironically, in this instance if the information about the behavior of the district staff were made public, it seems likely to further diminish the likelihood of success of future tax levies! Political issues aside, however, the point we wish to make here is that the behavior of school personnel can be unpredictable.

If there is one important broad point to be found in the preceding example, it probably is that exchange relationships need to balance the perceived inputs and perceived outcomes of individuals involved, and that it may be very difficult to assess what the perceptions of the individuals involved actually are. Possibilities that appear to be clearly in the best interests of some of the involved parties may not seem that way to the participants. A second point that may be worth considering is that smaller and decentralized school districts may provide better opportunities for research than larger, centralized ones. Third, the example above illustrates that time lines can be at best unpredictable, which should be considered if one's own time is limited.

Earlier in this section we alluded to the types of resources that might be used to facilitate access to school populations. At this point, we will suggest in more detail types of resources that could be viewed as valuable by school personnel: First, there are many situations in which schools need help developing specific types of programs. In such circumstances, you might be able to assist behind the scenes as a consultant or adviser. Second, schools are always looking for meaningful staff development activities; providing either in-service workshops or money to support such workshops can be a major incentive. Third, assistance to teachers is a resource that is always in short supply. Providing replacement instruction or your own teachers to implement the interventions that you are using offers a breather for classroom teachers. If you don't have access to replacement teachers or funds for substitutes, an alternative is to go into the classes as a resource person and lead sessions on topics about which you are an expert. Fourth, many teachers want to expand their skills, so if you are working with new techniques, it may be sufficient to teach those techniques to the teachers as you use them. Fifth, there may be some relatively modest ways of meaningfully representing your appreciation, like sending letters to administrators acknowledging the efforts of participating staff, taking staff members out to lunch or hosting an after-school get-together, or giving them token gifts that acknowledge their contributions and efforts.

In conclusion, it is important that you view the resources we have described as suggestions that may or may not be needed and may or may not be valued. Once again, through contact with school staff you may readily find out about modest needs in areas in which you can help, and the help you give can be a springboard to increased cooperation and appreciation. Finally, even if you are given carte blanche over what you do and asked for nothing in return, acknowledging your appreciation in some way is likely an important symbolic gesture and one that can be of major benefit for future requests and efforts by you or by other researchers.

TIME

We conclude this chapter with some issues of time. We already have spoken about the need to spend time familiarizing yourself with the sites and talking with staff, and you may be wondering, given all this preparation, how long the research will likely take. Even though the answer "there are no simple answers" undoubtedly sounds like one used by parents and intentionally obfuscatory college professors, it unfortunately is the best we can do, for it is true. For those of you who want something more concrete, however, we provide the time lines we used for our study of 31 schools (see Table 3.2), covering the first year of our project. Table 3.2 contains a description of each activity listed by the month that it was slated to be completed. Readers can get some sense of the changes that we were forced to make by noting which activities had been successfully completed by mid-spring of the year (see the left column). Our time line likely represents, however, an upper-end estimate, for it involved numerous sites and was slated to occur over a three-year period. We attempted to give ourselves plenty of time to prepare, as we knew that developing instruments, pretesting them, and then duplicating and distributing them would be a major undertaking.

Do not assume that school research can be started just any time during the year. As the time line in Table 3.2 reflects, there are patterns to the school year that suggest particular starting times and schedules for

Table 3.2
Evaluation Event Chart

Objective Completed	Year 1 (1987-1988)
September	
Yes	1-1. Organization of research activities for studies 1-5, with review of research design and data collection systems, and delineation of responsibilities.
Yes	1-2. Identification of schools for study 1.
Yes	1-3. Identification of 60 students from each school for achievement testing. (2,700 students were tested.)
Yes	1-4. Identification of research assistants.
Yes	1-5. Development of School Effectiveness Measures (SEM; now called School Characteristics Survey, or SCharS).
No	1-6. Fall evaluation meeting. (Not warranted because project was still in the organizational stages.)
October	
Yes	2-1. Begin achievement testing of 60 students. (Began in January.)
Yes	2-2. Begin collecting data on SEM1 (mail out information and/or conduct interviews). (Began in January.)
November	
Yes	3-1. Complete achievement testing.
Yes	3-2. Complete data collection on SEM1 (follow-up mailings/phone calls, finish interviews).
December	
Yes	4-1. Score and code achievement test data.
Yes	4-2. Begin coding and analyses of data from SEM1.
January	
Yes	5-1. Complete coding and analyses for SEM1.
No	5-2. Begin data collection (mailings and interviews) for SEM2. (Will begin in April.)
Yes	5-3. Development of classroom observation of structure form.
February	
No	6-1. Selection of comparison schools based on fall data for further project participation.
No	6-2. Complete data collection for SEM2.
Yes	6-3. Training of staff for achievement testing and administration of Curriculum-Based Measures (CBM). (Used Basic Academic Skill Samples.)
March	
Yes	7-1. Begin coding and analysis of data from SEM2.
No	7-2. Begin data collection for SEM3. (Will only be conducted twice.)

continued

Table 3.2

Evaluation Event Chart (*Continued*)

Objective Completed	Year 1 (1987-1988)
Yes	7-3. Begin identification of low-achieving 10% of students in reading using standardized achievement tests and CBM in Target and Comparison Schools.
Yes	7-4. Begin identification of all MH and LD students not identified in #3 above from Target and Comparison Schools.
No	7-5. Field testing of classroom observation structure form.
April	
No	8-1. Begin achievement posttesting of 60 student participants.
No	8-2. Complete coding and analysis of data from SEM2.
No	8-3. Complete data collection for SEM3.
No	8-4. Complete ID of 10% low-achieving, LD, and MH students in Target and Comparison Schools.
No	8-5. Collection of IEPs for identified students.
No	8-6. Collection of marker variable information for low-achieving, LD, and MH students.
May	
No	9-1. Complete achievement testing.
No	9-2. Begin coding and analysis of SEM3.
No	9-3. Begin analysis of coding of IEPs.
No	9-4. Complete collection of marker variables.
June	
No	10-1. Score and code achievement test data.
No	10-2. Complete coding and analysis of SEM3.
No	10-3. Complete coding and analysis of IEPs.
No	10-4. Analysis of marker variable data.
No	10-5. Begin analysis of data from Year 1.
Yes	10-6. Spring evaluation meeting.
July	
No	11-1. Complete analysis of Year 1 data.
No	11-2. Report writing.
August	
No	12-1. Report writing.
No	12-2. Year 2 planning.

research activities. We will address time lines in more detail in Chapter 9, but we will broadly sketch some concerns here. First, assume that obtaining access will be facilitated by starting conversations with school staff early, for example, during the preceding school year.

Second, avoid burdening school staff at the very beginning and end of school years. Third, we have found the best time for implementing interventions to be between January and the spring break; even though this period includes the two February holidays and parent-teacher conferences (with school closed to provide teachers with compensation time to make up for time spent in conferences with parents), it is preferable to fall, when there are professional teacher conferences, Thanksgiving and Christmas breaks, and additional parent-teacher conferences.

Issues of time provide yet another illustration of the importance of working collaboratively with school staff; you must meet the needs of all participants if you are to develop a schedule and intervention that has a fair chance of working. Be sure to sit down with people familiar with the schedule and behavior patterns of the school, so they can tell you how reasonable your planned time line is and what potential problems you might encounter.

EXERCISE

6. *Characteristics of Good Teachers.* Think about what you believe characterizes good teachers and bad teachers. Are those characterizations derived from specific individuals you had as teachers or others around you had? Compare your views with those of others in your class. Are there marked differences between recollections of those of you with children in school compared with those of you who have had few recent contacts with schools? Are there regional differences among you in what and how you recall your schooling? Are there other factors (gender, ethnicity/race, age, social class, public vs. private schooling, etc.) that seem to be related to major or important differences in student perceptions? In wrapping up this exercise, examine the range of different perceptions and think about the implications of those differences in what you look for in and expect from schools.

4

Issues of Design, Sampling, and Analysis

In this chapter we review research issues related to design, sampling, and analysis. Since such issues are covered in detail by numerous books on research methods (see, e.g., Cook & Campbell, 1979; Hedrick, Bickman, & Rog, in press; Henry, 1990; Judd, Smith, & Kidder, 1990), we will not try to summarize those issues here. Rather, we will attempt to view them from perspectives specific to school-based research. In particular, we will discuss issues of design, appropriate levels of data aggregation for conducting data analyses, how to review practical aspects of your treatments, sampling issues, meeting necessary standards for subject participation (i.e., informed consent), and how to anticipate and begin to address issues of subject attrition. Unfortunately, the topics covered in this chapter tend to be technical and complex. Thus, some of the discussions will likely exceed the level of preparation of some readers. To assist you in managing the material, near the end of each technical section we restate its important principles.

DESIGNING THE STUDY

As you have already decided what you want to do and where you want to do it, you should have already dealt with issues of design. But your decisions should not be closed to reconsideration, and this may be a good time to review what you plan to do now that you have a much better idea about constraints that are likely to be imposed on your study. Your experiences with your particular schools very likely will lead you to rethink your design. Our discussion of design issues will separately address experimental, quasi-experimental, and nonexperimental designs. For all three areas we are assuming for sake of simplicity that quantitative data are collected. We will leave issues related to fidelity of treatment and potential concerns about implementation of the treatments for a later chapter.

Experimental Design

Experimental research includes all studies in which subjects are randomly assigned to the different conditions of interest. Because of random assignment, differences found between subject responses to the various conditions should be attributable to the manipulations rather than to extraneous variables. That is, ideally the different groups are equivalent on all variables except their exposure to the independent variable(s). Because the only differences between conditions are the independent variables, experiments should be able to assess causal impact of those variables on the dependent measures of interest. *Only* experiments can disentangle issues of cause and effect, but even with experiments results can be misinterpreted. If the manipulations inadvertently vary other variables concurrently with the variables of interest, alternative interpretations of the findings are possible.

Experiments are well suited for assessing the respective worth of two different treatments on a sample of subjects. For example, if we wanted to examine how quickly students learned when they used cooperative learning methods versus individualistic ones, we could randomly assign the participants to the two different conditions, impose the manipulation, and compare the rates of learning.

For work done in educational settings, experimental designs are complicated by the need to consider the level at which subjects are assigned to conditions. If subjects participate within their classes, one needs to judge whether and how the class could have affected individual responses. The issue becomes whether entire classes rather than individual students should be assigned to treatments. In part, that issue may be answered through the following questions: Will you be allowed to take all the student participants and randomly assign them to conditions, or will you have to work with intact classes? Will you split each class into subgroups? These two questions are important, for even if you begin your study assuming that you will use random assignment, you may find that classes simply cannot be reconfigured. Particularly if all students in any class receive a single treatment, there are dangers that the findings could somehow be influenced by extraneous differences between classes (i.e., that assignment to conditions really was not random) or reflect dynamics specific to one or a few classes. In particular, there are potential problems if dynamics of particular classes shape the outcomes of all students in those classes rather than each student being independently affected by the treatments (in the language of research design, the assumption about independence of observations is violated).

Even though concerns about extraneous variables are present in any experimental study, the relatively large number of subjects that come from a single classroom with its own unique idiosyncracies make the problem in educational research larger than in a typical experimental study. Furthermore, the criteria schools use to assign students to classes almost always reflect some systematic biases rather than randomness, which can make the distinction between experimental and quasi-experimental research a tenuous one. For example, assignment of elementary students to particular teachers may be shaped by factors such as parental requests, principal beliefs (e.g., principals may believe that certain teachers are particularly adept at or incapable of working with certain types of students), or teacher preferences. Further, if elective classes and activities are available, self-selection of students into those electives (e.g., band, debate, sports), particularly at the secondary level, can limit their availability for assignment to other classes. Thus, assignment to those other classes can become nonrandom, and researchers can reestablish random assignment only if they employ subject selection randomized within classes.

Whenever intact classes are used, the most conservative way to minimize extraneous effects is to balance classes as much as possible across conditions and then to use the class as the level of analysis (i.e., use each class's average response as a single observation for the analyses). Such an approach obviously is very costly and time consuming, as the sample size becomes one unit for each class; the cost can be diminished somewhat if a subsample of students from each class is selected for inclusion in the study (selecting a representative subsample typically requires random selection of students within each class). An alternative that makes use of individual data yet examines the effects of class is to use classes and subjects within classes as variables in the experimental design. Such an approach is more complicated both in design and analyses, however, and does not seem to be very frequently chosen. In such instances, the same number of participants needs to be selected from each class. Then, in the statistical analyses of the Analysis of Variance model, class becomes a variable (typically nested within treatments, unless all treatments occur in each class) with students nested within class. In general, treatment effects are compared to their interaction with subjects within classes. (For determining the exact statistical tests for a particular design, see, e.g., Winer, 1971.)

Stratification is a second issue to consider for experimental research. This term refers to subdividing the sample before randomly assigning subjects to conditions and then, within subgroups, randomly assigning individuals to conditions. Stratification can be important when there are demographic or background variables that need to be considered because they may bias your findings. Stratification is appropriate if you worry about questions like: Do I need to have the same proportion of boys and girls in each condition? Would I feel more comfortable about my study if I randomly assigned subjects to conditions within gender or ability level or ethnic/racial background? For example, a researcher may be interested in effectiveness of a particular treatment when implemented in groups of students that are heterogeneous with respect to academic ability. If so, the treatment conditions likely need to be set up to assure that certain minimum numbers of children of "high," "moderate," and "low" academic ability are in each group. In such circumstances, stratified sampling assures that each group contains the appropriate mix of students.

Researchers who work in educational settings frequently collect data on demographic variables (e.g., ethnic/racial background, gender) in case they later decide they want to or need to use those data for post hoc analyses. If there are important research questions that involve such variables, a priori stratification of subjects on the demographic variables will provide a much better means of testing research questions about those variables.

Regardless of how students are assigned to conditions, school-based experimental research encounters additional concerns that demand special consideration. Those considerations encompass a range of issues, including ones related to our earlier discussion of nonrandomness introduced due to prior interactions among subjects or stemming from unwanted interactions among students within and across treatment conditions. Each of these issues requires careful planning before and during the research. In addition, as noted earlier, unusual dynamics or events unrelated to the treatments occurring within one or a few of the classrooms used in a study may have a powerful impact on the outcomes and warrant particular attention.

Finally, certain types of research done in educational settings are much more amenable to use of random assignment than are others. For example, social science researchers conducting theoretically oriented research within school settings should be better able to design randomized experiments than researchers who conduct research on educational intervention or innovation, which requires implementation of treatments within entire classrooms.

Quasi-Experimental Design

Quasi-experimental research is similar to experimental research in form, but lacks either randomized assignment of subjects to conditions or a controlled manipulation. Quasi-experimental research is very common in educational settings, for in many instances research in schools simply cannot be designed to impose the controls necessary to create a true experiment. Many studies of program implementation cannot find comparable treatment and comparison schools. For example, if one wishes to test the effectiveness of an early reading intervention, the sample of classrooms would have to be matched based on the techniques currently in use and the backgrounds of the children. All too often, finding comparable classes willing to participate in research is virtually impossible, which forces researchers to accept a quasi-experimental design as the most viable way of conducting the research.

Furthermore, many pretest / intervention /posttest studies that initially are designed to be experiments often end up encountering problems that compromise the integrity of the treatment and make them quasi-experimental. In such instances, the research that is done may resemble an experiment, but lack the controls (e.g., random assignment, equivalence of the control group) of experimental research.

For an example of a quasi-experimental research design, we return again to our study of children with mild disabilities: That study was designed from the outset as a quasi-experiment, for we knew we would be unable to exercise sufficient control over the ways that the theoretical programs were implemented by the various sites to assure comparability across sites. In addition, we had no way of establishing equivalence of the various schools, for they had their own histories, student populations, teachers, facilities, and programs. Some were urban, others suburban, others in small towns or rural. Student turnover varied widely across schools. (Parallel arguments about between-site differences could be made even for any cross-building comparisons within a single district unless that school district implements totally random busing programs.)

Even though it is more difficult to draw reliable inferences from quasi-experimental research than from experimental research, quasi-experimental designs do allow researchers to investigate questions that cannot feasibly be investigated experimentally. For example, they allow investigations of questions like: What are the social status effects of homogeneously and heterogeneously grouped classrooms? What are the effects of dietary nutrition on school achievement? How do private schools compare to public schools? How does school district size or school size relate to student learning? How does the presence of a strong private school system affect the public schools in a community? How does the size of the community relate to student social development? The number of questions may be endless. (Note, however, the difficulty in unambiguously determining cause and effect from such research.)

Like studies that compare different types of schools, interventions that are implemented broadly (e.g., state-mandated or federally regulated changes) cannot be investigated experimentally. In these cases, the design is necessarily quasi-experimental because all schools typically change at the same point in time, leaving no untreated control group. (Note that true experiments may be possible if exceptions are made for particular schools or programs within schools.) In instances where all schools simultaneously undergo change, the pre-post comparisons cannot control for a number of threats to validity like history (events that occur between testings), maturation (processes within subjects that occur with the passage of time, like growing older), and so forth (for a complete description of threats to validity, see Campbell & Stanley, 1963). In such instances it probably is worth trying to locate untreated comparison groups even if those groups differ somewhat from the experimental groups.

One final point to consider when discussing quasi-experimental research is the dangers of what are called regression artifacts for matched-group comparisons. Matched groups are used to establish comparability of two or more different groups at a particular point in time. For example, we might select groups of boys and girls who have comparable mathematics skills at the beginning of a research project. In instances where the matches are drawn from nonequivalent populations, however, the matching will be flawed unless the measure on which the individuals are matched provides a perfectly reliable and valid representation of the dimension on which the individuals are selected. In the absence of perfect reliability and validity, your groups will not be accurately matched.

Classic examples of wrong inferences drawn due to regression artifacts are provided in the Head Start literature. Numerous studies matched Head Start participants on achievement level with other children drawn from more affluent and enriched populations. On retesting, the comparison subjects frequently appeared to have improved more than Head Start participants due simply to effects of regression toward the mean, and once regression effects were removed, the findings changed markedly (see, e.g., Campbell & Erlebacher, 1970). The point is that both imprecision in assessing the underlying dimension of interest and unreliability of measures of that dimension can result in selecting two groups that really are not equivalent; on subsequent measures they will diverge toward their respective population means regardless of any effects of treatment. Furthermore, the more extreme the discrepancy of the selected group from its population mean, the greater the overall movement of that group back toward the population mean on subsequent assessments (for a discussion of regression artifacts, see Thorndike, 1942). Most important for current readers is to be aware that even though matching of subjects seems attractive, there are potential difficulties that are complex. They will be difficult to understand unless one has a strong grounding in regression techniques and reliability theory.

Nonexperimental Design

Nonexperimental designs are those that either lack a manipulation or do not permit assessment of the impact of any manipulations that occur. They therefore can speak only speculatively about cause and effect. They encompass a range of types of research, including correlational/prediction, and one-shot single-group designs. Most correlational research lacks a treatment, so comparisons of different groups identify relationships between variables, yet are silent about the causal dynamics underlying those relationships. In one-shot single-group designs, researchers find themselves attempting to draw inferences from data collected from a single group at a single point in time. In such situations, perhaps the best that can be done is to see whether the data are consistent with theoretical predictions and compare the findings with existing norms or outcomes from other research.

As is true for all types of research, analyses of nonexperimental research typically begin with descriptive statistics, which provide context and background for inferential analyses. Inferential analyses, relying on comparisons of means, on correlations, or on the family of regression approaches, attempt to address questions derived from conceptual models of interest.

As an illustration, think again of our study of low-achieving students. Initial descriptive analyses allowed us to determine whether the assumptions of parametric analyses were met (i.e., did the distributions of the variables approximate a normal curve) and also to provide other researchers with data they can use to compare their populations with ours. Note for example that a Minnesota sample including a number of rural schools is likely to have fewer nonwhite subjects than one from a geographic area with a more heterogeneous population, and that the low-achieving children may be at higher or lower achievement levels than low-achieving children from other studies.

For inferential analyses, imagine that we were trying to draw inferences about a single intervention without a control group. In such an instance, group comparison approaches would not work, for we have only a single group. As ways of attempting to draw inferences, we could (a) look at correlations of variables that measure the effectiveness of the intervention with student outcomes (if outcomes were positively related to measures of the effectiveness of the intervention, we could argue that our treatment seemed to work); (b) compare growth rates with those reported by other studies or in comparable populations, using, for example, archival data from student files to provide a baseline and to allow some crude measures of growth (finding growth rates seemingly comparable to or exceeding those of other studies would provide support for our treatment); and (c) use variables discussed in (a) along with some traditional predictors of achievement to try to predict student performance (if the measures of effectiveness add to the explanatory power of the other variables, we could again argue for the usefulness of our treatment).

If data are collected at more than one point in time, most likely before and after some treatment or intervention, the study can be considered quasi-experimental; this pre-post design is discussed in methods books following the Campbell and Stanley (1963) tradition. Thus, there are opportunities to broaden the analyses to address more experiment-like questions. For example, there then should be available real measures of growth, provided the same measures are collected at each point in time. Such multiple-point analyses have variously been called repeated measures, panel, multiwave, or longitudinal analyses. These analyses are much more powerful than single-point analyses, for they allow the performance levels of individuals prior to treatment to be used as a baseline for measuring growth. For prediction analyses like regression techniques, inclusion of the prior measure of a variable that is being predicted yields an estimate of stability and, thus, allows us to assess incremental impacts of other predictor variables. (Longitudinal analyses will be discussed in more detail in a later chapter of this book.)

In summary, nonexperimental analyses provide alternative means for assessing the effectiveness of educational interventions. Even though they cannot provide direct tests of the effectiveness of those interventions, they can provide corroborating information and help direct future experimental research. In effect, experimental, quasi-experimental, and nonexperimental research complement each other and all are useful in educational settings. Educational research benefits from multiple approaches in the same way that theoretical research benefits from multiple operationalizations of variables, namely, through the convergence of different approaches each having its own strengths and shortcomings.

AGGREGATION AND ANALYSIS

One of the major challenges for research in educational settings is to find the most appropriate level at which to analyze the data. For example, school effectiveness research could use as its single observation or unit of analysis individuals (how are particular individuals affected), classes (how are classes affected), or buildings (how do changes affect entire schools). Because the issue of choosing the appropriate unit of analysis is so critical, we introduced it early on and have already referred to it several times; it can provide a major disincentive to conducting educational research.

For many researchers and even more reviewers, the most appropriate unit of analysis is the most conservative one, for at that level there is little danger of being too optimistic in one's conclusions. At the same time, a conservative view may be so demanding that it all but eliminates educational research, for it typically requires massive loss of data through aggregation. For example, research that requires collecting data on every child from an entire school in order to yield a single data point (e.g., the average school achievement score) is terribly cost-ineffective and discourages educational research.

Fortunately, however, there are few instances in which major data loss is necessary; if building-level data are needed, to minimize the amount of data collected, typically only random sampling within buildings is done. In some instances, data can be analyzed at different levels depending upon the questions that are being asked. The other extreme from major data aggregation is the one in which individual-level data are analyzed, totally ignoring schools or classes. Unfortunately, even when the focus is on the behavior of individuals, ignoring broader contexts allows errors of inference insofar as results are due to idiosyncracies of or uncontrolled variables operating in specific groups.

There are no simple answers to the question of the appropriate level of data aggregation. Methodological and statistical sophistication can compensate for some problems, but the most credible results are those that do not need to be sanitized by complicated statistical procedures. Imposing statistical controls may help data sets address questions that otherwise are beyond their scope, but such controls increase the likelihood of investigator errors, can make the results incomprehensible to practitioners, and require researchers to make additional assumptions that may not be true. For example, consider a technique like analysis of covariance, which is commonly used when other controls are not available. Analysis of covariance attempts to control statistically for preexisting differences so the final outcomes of the various groups can be compared. Imagine that we want to control for class effects and a pretest score in examining the relation of treatment to a posttest score. To understand what the adjusted score means, one needs to understand how covariance works, needs to be able to generate dummy variables for class, and needs to have a perfectly reliable measure as the pretest. Furthermore, many statistical packages do not provide residual scores, which means that such scores have to be calculated by the investigator, which introduces another possibility for error, particularly since the pattern of the residual scores may be very unlike the pattern of the unadjusted scores. In short, there is no substitute for keeping things simple and addressing the questions of interest in as direct a fashion as is possible.

Consider again our study of low-achieving children. We sampled six children from each class, and then used their responses in examining the benefits of the different treatments on children's outcomes. For some analyses, we looked also at grade in school, in others at building, and in yet others at gender, at special education status, and at other potentially relevant variables. Because our design was quasi-experimental, we needed to look at the data in many ways so we could attempt to tease apart extraneous effects from those in which we were interested (recognizing that we never would be able to speak definitively because the study was not experimental). Other analyses were done at the class level, for we also were interested in questions that embedded the approaches within contextual variables reflecting school effectiveness and climate. For those analyses we aggregated the responses of children within each class, yielding one score on each measure at the class level, and then linked those scores with the responses of teachers on our measures of climate.

As we hope readers have deduced from the preceding ideas and examples, researchers by their research questions define an appropriate level at which to collect and analyze the data. In addition, in many ways educational researchers become detectives, trying to uncover clues about how and why things happen the way they do. The goal is to examine the data from a number of different perspectives, attempting to see whether the inferences stay the same regardless of the perspective, and then, if the inferences differ, attempting to determine the perspective with which one feels most comfortable.

From our perspective, liberal data exploration coupled with conservative interpretation of the findings can provide an approach that takes advantage of available data without abusing the scientific process. Note that we are not advocating atheoretical exploration of the data, but instead suggesting the addressing of questions of interest in multiple ways. Just because you have found one way to answer the question that interested you does not mean that you can quit. Look for other ways, then see whether the answer to the question stays the same.

SAMPLE SELECTION

Understanding principles of sampling is another skill that educational researchers should possess. Fortunately, the Sage Applied Social Research Methods Series includes a book on applied sampling issues (Henry, 1990); basic questions should be answered in that source or others like it. Several important issues related to sampling and subject selection recur commonly in educational research; some are found in much applied research, but others seem idiosyncratic to educational settings. These issues warrant attention, particulary when making decisions about the scope of a study or the bases for selecting participants. In this section, we will discuss defining the subject population, obtaining consent, and dealing with attrition.

Defining the Subject Population

Much of the research done in educational settings has as its focus specific target groups. For example, our research on students with mild disabilities focused on the subset of children falling into that category. At the same time, however, we still were interested in being able to put the experiences of that group into the broader context of what was happening within the entire class, so we also had to consider sampling from other children who were not part of that group.

In addition, even focusing only within the group of low-achieving children, we were faced with the issue of whether we should draw a homogeneous sample of low-achieving children (e.g., only the very lowest children in each class; or only children given a special education services label by the school) or a more heterogeneous sample (e.g., by conducting our own testing and drawing from a broader pool of students who scored below the norms for their age group). One of the issues here parallels the one above: If we sample homogeneously we will be able to focus our energies on a smaller and more clearly defined group, but our conclusions would be limited to that group. That is, our findings might be less generalizable if we sample more narrowly. Being able to draw only limited conclusions may be fine for theoretical development, but for policy decisions a limited sample seems less valuable, particularly if the recommended approaches would work as well on a broader group of children. It can be helpful to collect comparison data so policymakers can better judge the broad implications (i.e., on all low-achieving children, on the entire classroom, and potentially, on the entire school) of targeted interventions.

Returning again to our study of low-achieving children, we needed to balance the advantages of a more representative sample with the disadvantages of having to track progress of and interact with a larger and diverse sample. We decided to define *low-achieving* fairly broadly (incidentally, school differences that emerged in how and when particular labels were used confirmed the soundness of our decision not to use school-assigned labels), and we collected data on other children besides those of primary interest. As we were working in a dozen schools and had limited time available to collect and analyze data, we chose to collect only limited measures from the higher-achieving children, to sample a lesser proportion of them, and to leave their data for later analyses. We made this decision reluctantly because it limited our conclusions and potentially could have left us with a finding or findings that we could not understand, but we simply did not have the resources to follow and monitor students across the entire achievement continuum on the full array of measures that we were collecting.

Integrally related to issues of sampling are issues of data analysis. Most important, if we sample only low-achieving children, we are a priori restricting the range of scores on virtually all measures of achievement. Obviously, restriction of range lessens correlations of achievement variables with other variables. One instance in which achievement variables are unrelated to or, in some instances, even show "backward" relations with traditional predictor variables is in predicting college success in programs designed for students who have done poorly in high school (often called special, experimental, or conditional admissions programs). In such programs, the high school grade point averages (GPAs) of all students are low (otherwise they would not be in special admissions programs), and consequently, GPA is a poorer predictor of college performance in that sample than across the full array of college admissions.

A second issue that emerges in sampling from only a portion of a broader distribution of scores is whether the relationships between variables operate in the same way in that part of the continuum as elsewhere. For example, one of the issues that universities and colleges face in admitting students who perform poorly on traditional predictors of college success is how to use such predictors. If the predictors operate the same as they do for the full range of scores, then predictors like GPA and standardized test scores should predict success within such programs. But if such measures do not accurately reflect whatever factors distinguish graduates from dropouts, then alternative measures need to be used. Note that the point is that in some instances, the nature of the relationship between variables is not changed, but only less obvious due to the restricted range. In other instances, the relationship may actually differ for people from various parts of the distribution. Perhaps the practical issue is to consider potential consequences of different patterns before collecting the data so alternative measures are considered and the findings are viewed from a range of perspectives.

Further complicating the issue of sampling are questions about whether the sampling has excluded subjects who ought to be included or included subjects who ought to be excluded; both types of errors reflect inaccuracies in classification techniques. Additional arguments suggest that in some instances subjects might not end up where they belong due to idiosyncracies, randomness, or other factors. If such nonselection is nonrandom, there can be problems with the interpretability of results. The most complex and sophisticated treatment of this last topic is provided by literature from sociology (see, e.g., Berk & Ray, 1982); because the principles are difficult to explain without an extended and technical explanation, we will not discuss them further here. For present purposes, it is sufficient to understand that any time a researcher chooses to sub-sample students above or below some cutoff point, the possibility of biasing is introduced.

Again our study of low-achieving children provides a straightforward example. Clearly, there is ambiguity in categorizing low-achieving children. Subcategories that are not necessarily discrete, like mildly mentally handicapped, learning disabled, emotionally disturbed, and slow learner create additional potential for inconsistency and even errors in classification, particularly across sites. One school, for example, had such a high proportion of economically disadvantaged and ethnic-minority children who did poorly on traditional indicators of academic progress that we might reasonably have applied one or more of the categories to almost every student in the school if we had used those categories as they were employed in other schools. As noted earlier, from the beginning it was clear to us that we could not simply use the labels that individual schools gave to their children. We collected data on the categories assigned but also used our own diagnostic instrument to obtain additional information.

To summarize briefly, issues of selection warrant consideration on technical, conceptual, and statistical grounds. Once again, careful planning can lessen the risk of unpleasant surprises in both what you actually find and how others critique your work.

Obtaining Consent

Earlier we described the relationship between researchers and schools as an exchange in which each group benefits. Arranging the basic relationship so both groups are pleased will provide the framework for achieving informed consent, but there still may be specific forms to be completed and kept on file for you to proceed (for a full review of issues of consent, see Sieber, 1992). Note that we say "may be," for policies can vary greatly from school to school. If the study is instructional and the measures are similar to those collected as part of regular instruction, your assurance of subject anonymity may be all that is needed. If, however, you wish to collect additional measures, in many instances the parents may need to sign a form stating their approval.

As noted above, if the staff supports your research, the principals and teachers may be willing to become involved in development of the consent forms and even send a cover letter along with the form. Such letters are valuable to you because they can lessen the apprehension of parents and increase the participation rate. Problems arise from the carelessness of students who lose the consent forms, parents who are so busy that they forget about the forms, or general resistance to change and innovation. We have found no foolproof solution, but one option is to provide some type of incentive for parents or children. For example, children can be told that once a certain number of response forms are returned, they then will be able to engage in specific activities (note that it is helpful if some aspect of the study is considered to be "fun" or engaging so that children want to participate). Individual incentives also work, but may get a lesser proportion of respondents than if peers are encouraging one another to get the forms filled in and returned. A second option, which can be used along with incentives, is to divide participants into teams that "compete" to see who is fastest in returning the forms. Competitions have a downside of stigmatizing the children who are unable to return the forms quickly, however. Finally, in some instances "negative" consent forms are allowed. In that case, students can participate unless the nonconsent form is returned denying permission to participate. Many human subjects review panels frown upon this practice, because it is not clear that consent actually has been given.

In concluding this section, we should note that sample attrition due to not returning consent forms is seldom random, and in case of appreciable attrition you should review the research literature mentioned above about selection biases. Although the particular biases may change markedly depending upon the type of study and the relationships of the researchers with school personnel and community leaders, in general lower-class and ethnic-minority students tend to yield lower response rates.

Attrition in Longitudinal Research

The final issue to be addressed in this chapter is subject attrition. In the above discussions, we have attempted to integrate issues of attrition with other issues, but attrition involves much more than, for example, losing subjects who forget to fill out consent forms, and comes from a range of sources. We attempt here to cover the major sources of attrition to help you in considering how attrition may affect the number of subjects required at the beginning of a study and the types of conclusions that can reasonably be drawn from the sample that is obtained. Nonparticipation has already been discussed; we continue with missing data, absenteeism, geographic relocation, school reorganization, and nonpromotion.

In almost all research settings, participants make mistakes. Random omissions are one source of problems, for example, when a participant accidentally skips one item on a questionnaire. Such problems may not be major, for average scores can be computed and used to replace the missing score when a small proportion of item responses is missing. Alternatively, estimates of missing data can be calculated using regression techniques to predict how the subject will respond (we recommend consulting a statistician here). In some instances, the mean of the respondent or of the sample for the omitted item will suffice. A more difficult type of omission comes when some participants forget, for example, to go on to the back of the form or skip an entire section of the form. Most problematic are items that are purposely skipped by some portion of the participants, for example because they are viewed as sensitive, as incomprehensible, or as reactive. In these last two instances, it is difficult to estimate with any degree of accuracy what the missing responses are likely to be. In the last case, the items clearly have nonrandom loss, compromising even the available data. Finally, there is an additional source of data loss in the failure of teachers or schools to administer measures when they are supposed to be administered or from their losing the information once it is collected. Such failures result in massive data loss. For example, one site from our study of low-achieving children supposedly sent a set of our measures to another university with whom they had previously collaborated; we have not ever found those measures and lost an entire school for some of our analyses.

A second source of attrition is absenteeism. Children may get sick or travel with their family just when we decide to collect data. Again unfortunately, absenteeism is not random; some children are sick more often than others, some have travel opportunities that most others don't, some absentees reflect truancies, and yet other children may be absent because they have to take care of younger siblings who are sick. In practice, most absences reflect nonrandom factors that cause problems for drawing inferences from the remaining data.

A third type of attrition arises from children moving away from the school during the school year. Even though some loss is to be expected with the prevailing patterns of geographic mobility, there is additional movement unrelated to job changes. Only a very small proportion of this change comes from families that own homes moving to other homes, and that movement often is planned to occur during the summer. Larger changes arise from the economic instability of families of low socioeconomic status, which often move around the first and fifteenth of any month. Even school policies that keep children in the same school regardless of changes of residence within a school district do little good in areas where school districts are small and cross-city movement is common. For these circumstances, you might remind yourself that your problems are minimal compared to the havoc that cross-school movement plays with the educational progress of those children. For researchers, the harsh fact is that in a typical desegregated school you will undoubtedly find greater attrition among lower-class and minority students, so if you are interested in those students you had better plan to oversample them, that is, include more of them in your sample than you ultimately want so that after attrition you have remaining a sufficient sample. For example, one of us was involved in a school desegregation study that encountered severe attrition problems. For some longitudinal analyses, complete data were available on only 136 of 711 white children (19%) sampled across the 4-year period used as the time frame for the analyses. Attrition rates for both Mexican-American and African-American students were even higher and the initial samples smaller, yielding insufficient numbers of students for comparable analyses. Our study of low-achieving children showed comparable patterns, with highest attrition in the urban schools.

Another source of subject attrition is school reorganization. The broadest impact comes from changes like reorganizing attendance zones and programs, which can require researchers to follow children who began in a single school as they disperse across a number of schools. Again, our study of low-achieving children provides a concrete example: One of our schools closed at the end of the first year of our study. Fortunately for us, the children were reassigned to other schools that were part of our study. School-option programs can produce comparable results on a smaller scale as students choose to change programs or go from a neighborhood school to a magnet school. Public-to-private and private-to-public school transfers also occur, for example, when parents are dissatisfied with the progress of their children in their current schools.

Some types of reorganization within schools also can cause problems for researchers. For example, although the impacts of reconfiguring children within classrooms as they move from one grade to another seems potentially to have minimal effects on their achievement levels, disrupting friendship patterns can have adverse effects on individual children. Finally, for studies like ours that follow progress of low-achieving children, nonpromotion becomes a concern. Students who are not promoted provide a dilemma, for they are obviously getting different instruction than others of their age and formerly of their grade.

We have tried to make you aware of potential sources of attrition so you can plan for attrition and assure yourself of having a sufficient sample size at the end of your research. If you decide to do power analyses (see, e.g., Lipsey, 1990) to determine how many subjects you need in each condition, work backward, determining how many subjects you need to have remaining at the end of your study and increasing the sample size at each preceding time point consistent with your expectations of rates of attrition. If you expect differential attrition for various measures, attrition concerns may make you think differently about the measures that you want to collect. (Additional discussion of this last issue will be provided in the chapter about selection of measures.) Finally, nonrandomness of attrition warrants attention and discussion at the data analysis stage of your research.

EXERCISES

7. *Designing Educational Research.* In Exercise 3 at the end of Chapter 1, research hypotheses were generated. Develop (a) experimental, (b) quasi-experimental, and (c) nonexperimental studies to test those hypotheses. Working in groups of three or four, select two questions that are most interesting and that have the broadest impact. How many seem easier to address experimentally rather than using quasi-experimental or nonexperimental approaches? Why? Finally,

select one design and present it to the class. Critique each design, focusing on strengths as well as shortcomings. Propose alternatives to overcome shortcomings that you identify.

8. *Interpreting Findings From Quasi-Experimental Research.* Select the most interesting quasi-experimental designs from Exercise 7. What limits the conclusions that you might draw? What, for example, could you reasonably conclude about a comparison of public with private schools? What individual differences between students at the two types of schools likely would interfere with your attempts to talk about the consequences of the different types of schooling?

5

School Personnel: Committed, Indifferent, or Resistant

> *Teachers have tended to see themselves as victims. To me, that's incredibly ironic. They're terribly powerful. They can do anything they damn please when their door's closed. And yet they will complain about not having any control over the situation.*
>
> School board member quoted in Wahlstrom (1990, p. 280)

Now that the issues of sampling, consent, and analysis have been thought through and worked out, at least for the time being, it's time to think about other factors that can hinder us as we move on to conduct our study. In this chapter we focus on school personnel, most prominently teachers. The opening quotation captures the mixed role of teachers who, on one hand, may feel like they are helplessly carrying out the wishes of others but who, on the other hand, can completely determine the success of research projects.

One model for thinking about teachers' adoption of any innovation in their schools and classrooms is the Concerns-Based Adoption Model developed by Hall, George, and Rutherford (1979). Most important for our discussion, the model specifies that whenever teachers are asked to change their practices, their concerns follow a predictable pattern from "self" concerns (What does this mean for me?), to task concerns (How do I do this?), and then to "impact" concerns (What effects will this have on my students and colleagues?). The value of this model is that it reminds us as researchers that our focus is often quite different from the focus of the teachers with whom we are working. We are likely to focus our attention on teaching school staff how to implement a treatment and explaining the impact of the treatment on the students, perhaps inadequately addressing the teachers' self-concerns. They may then remain "stuck" at the self-concerned stage and never be able to effectively learn and implement the intervention or even consider how it can benefit them.

If we have been attentive to the concerns of teachers and others working with us, at this point in our study we hopefully will have worked out the basic quid pro quo of our study. As a result, all parties should be generally satisfied with (or at least accepting of) the arrangements and supportive of them. But if you are working with more than just the few school staff members most interested in and excited about the research, there is always the chance that some individuals will not be happy about what is going on and, consequently, will not do their best to help out. Here we attempt to describe different types of people you are likely to encounter in schools and strategies for working effectively with them. Thus, the discussion is only minimally directed at researchers who confine themselves to single classes; if you are working with only one or a few classes, then you may be fortunate and never encounter many of the issues covered here. For you, this chapter may only serve to build empathy for colleagues; when they come back to the Ivory Tower looking distraught, you'll be able to give them words of support and encouragement as you thank your lucky stars that they are the ones conducting complex, multiclass, multisite research.

Our goal in this chapter is not to be unsympathetic toward or make fun of teachers. In fact, there are good reasons why competent, dedicated school staff may be much less excited about research than are those of us in higher education. Thus, before we present our teacher "types," we attempt to provide outsiders with a rationale for why teachers might view research as a nuisance rather than an opportunity.

TEACHER ROLES AND RESPONSIBILITIES

When approached conscientiously, the role of teacher is a very demanding one. The responsibilities for organizing and managing activities are continuous and relentless—for at least 6 hours each day teachers are asked to create activities that engage the students, that keep them from becoming bored, and that help them to learn. Further, the typical partitioning of school days into 50-60-minute periods may not be particularly conducive to learning (see, e.g., Carroll, 1990). In addition, where typical jobs allow for discretionary use of time when needs arise (e.g., to make a phone call, use the bathroom, or even have a cup of coffee), teaching does not. Teachers are not free to leave their classrooms to attend to personal needs, for they can be held legally liable for damages incurred by students under their supervision, which demands their continual vigilance.

Thus, even without the demands of researchers, teachers often feel that they run a continuous juggling act. Our additional demands, no matter how small they seem to us, might place some of their other efforts in jeopardy. Our demands also compete with other recent pressures that reflect society's changing family and work patterns. For example, in virtually all schools teachers have been forced to adapt their behaviors in response to increases in the needs and demands of children whose parents are not at home during the day and may not have prepared them adequately for school. Given this array of responsibilities facing teachers, it perhaps should not be surprising to find some of them unenthusiastic about anything that complicates their lives any further, be it research and educational innovation or anything else.

Finally, despite teachers engaging in what they perceive as important efforts to provide care and nurturance to society's children, their profession nonetheless is granted relatively low status, at least in such visible measures as the level of compensation and the continuing public criticism of education. Add to these points one made earlier, that teacher training programs rarely teach teachers to expect to cooperate in doing research as a normal part of their jobs, and resistance to research becomes even easier to understand. But in fact, we have found many hard-working, capable, and very busy teachers who nonetheless are interested in participating in research efforts.

TEACHER TYPES

Given the heavy demands placed on teachers, implementation of your ideas may require intense negotiation between you and the school staff. The following hypothetical, if oversimplified, types of school staff are intended to help researchers to anticipate some of the ways school staff may respond to research overtures and understand the motivations that underlie those responses. In particular, we hope this discussion will help researchers (a) to recognize why they might be feeling frustrated and unappreciated by the people with whom they are working, and (b) to design constructive strategies for attaining research goals despite having to interact with school staff having far different needs than those of researchers.

First we present the "Ideal" teacher, the type of person who might make you find yourself thinking, "Wow, why did this person want to be a teacher. Someone this smart and committed should be a researcher like me." We should be careful to rein in our egocentrism, acknowledge that other people have different priorities than we do, and remember that we should not accept stereotypes regardless of what we read in newspapers about teachers. Second, there are the "Too Helpful" types who want to take over the study, or who want to do what they want to do rather than what we want to do, or who always have a better idea, or who change just a few things to help us out. Third are the "Overburdened" types, who already have too much to do and don't need any of our nonsense, particularly if we are so naive to believe that it will really make a difference. Fourth is the "Concrete Thinker," the person who needs continuous guidance and very specific advice on all the details of what needs to be done. This person reminds us that we researchers come from a unique, intellectually oriented Ivory Tower culture in which most others track verbally what we say and comprehend most of it, no matter how inelegantly we manage to articulate our ideas. Fifth is the "Passive Resister," who will never complain but will usually do what he or she can to keep us from getting what we need when we need it. Sixth is the "Crusty Veteran," who has seen more researchers come and go than you can shake a stick at, and is just getting too old to keep putting up with such silliness. As such individuals typically consider themselves to be leaders and spokespersons for their colleagues, their role is to tell naive outsiders like us what really is happening.

Clearly, these types border on caricatures. They are not intended to represent real individuals. Some teachers possess attributes from several types. In addition, variability in behavior across settings and time results in many teachers displaying characteristics of different types in differing amounts at different times, for example, sometimes cooperative, sometimes too helpful, sometimes bored, and sometimes unable to comprehend things that seem obvious to others.

Before we try to flesh out our types in more detail, it is important to put them in context. If a study begins with consultation, open discussion, and a development of mutual ownership of the research, we can expect that individual differences among staff members and their views of research will become less important. The investment of time at the beginning of the project should allow staff members to attain a broad understanding of the nature of the research and to exert their influence on its course before the study begins. The influence may be positive, improving design, or negative, as when sharp disagreements come out in the preliminary discussions and it becomes clear that the research would be better accomplished elsewhere. Once there has been an agreement about respective roles and responsibilities, you can hope that the staff will continue to support the project throughout its duration and immediately bring up any problems.

If you are perceived as open to reactions and input from school staff and if you seem to want the research experience to be beneficial to the staff as well as you, then you may substantially lessen any negative reactions and, equally important, receive social support from the staff. The most important aspects of the social support come from staff members transmitting the view that they personally support the research and will not sanction colleagues undermining it. Thus, you gain allies who know much better than you could what actually is going on and what needs to be done to keep the research on track.

In the ideal world, all school personnel are enthusiastic about research and work hard to support it. In the real world, an important goal is to approximate the ideal world, for doing so lessens the battles that will have to be fought and increases the likelihood that the research will get to an end close to the one envisioned. The practical value of our advice is captured in the comments of a superintendent talking about using resources to develop commitment in decision-making situations:

> I think you use extrinsic things (such as specific resources) to get certain programs to happen. . . . We barter when we set these things up. . . . [Once] the bartering's all over, we've made our deal. You *own* this thing now. Now the extrinsic is over, but the intrinsic is very important. . . . If you can get people beyond the bartering stage, . . . [you] get them into the intrinsic value of why they're there. . . . From the workplace, [the teachers need to get] a feeling like they are important and what they are doing is significant to the education of the child or that family. So, you can talk about resources all you want, and I use them, and I barter.
>
> Once that's all done, . . . if that teacher says, "Hey folks, we don't need that because we are who we are," I think you've got something intrinsic, [and] that makes that decision fly. (Wahlstrom, 1990, p. 145)

Finally, we should note that diversity among teacher types participating in a particular study is not necessarily bad. If the research question involves social contexts or requires that some approach be implemented widely (i.e., by all types of teachers), then diversity of teacher types may need to exist in the sample for the study to produce replicable results. In fact, teacher diversity even could be assessed and then analyzed as an independent variable in certain research projects.

The Ideal

The "Ideal" type is included here primarily to balance the more negative types that follow. Please note that by this discussion of negative types of school staff we do not mean to imply that as researchers you will be venturing into a necessarily hostile and antagonistic culture or that most of the stakeholders in that culture are going to cause you problems. Rather, you should recognize that all groups are diverse and note that certain types of diversity found with some degree of regularity among school personnel may create complexities that warrant forethought and preparation on your part.

Fortunately, there are many teachers and other school personnel who are enthusiastic about and supportive of research generally and will welcome yours in particular. It is to be hoped that you identified some supporters at the beginning of your project, for they can make it much easier for you to get even to this point. In the best of all worlds, they will have shepherded you through the idiosyncrasies of their schools, spoken up for your project in front of their colleagues, helped you learn how to fit your project into the school curriculum, and perhaps even conducted a pilot study in their classrooms (note, of course, that if you use them for a pilot study, they may not be able to participate in the broader study—unless you work across school years or with different classes that they have).

Ideal school staff are not a problem and in fact enrich the quality of your work, as they make it more pleasant. They can provide feedback, practical advice on subtle but important modifications of your design and its implementation, and insights into their culture. At his or her best, the ideal teacher is simultaneously a colleague, an adviser, and a guide. Without such individuals, your task becomes much more difficult and the chances of encountering severe problems much greater. In fact, for the ideal staff person, we can skip what will typically be the wrap-up of each of these sections, namely discussion of problems this type of teacher creates and how you might deal with them.

Too Helpful

The "Too Helpful" staff persons are perhaps the most difficult to deal with, mostly because those individuals resemble in many ways the ideal person and often view themselves as not only helpful but also an integral part of your research. In many instances, they have good intentions even though their disruptive behaviors produce bad results. For example, if their colleagues encounter problems, they may jump right in with their own ideas without consulting you ("I knew you were too busy to be bothered by such small details, and I knew we could handle it ourselves") and make changes that compromise the integrity of your treatment. They may believe they know what outcome you want and have better ideas about how to achieve those outcomes. They may even coach the students so that they perform as you would like them to perform. "Too helpfuls" may also like to tout what they are doing and tell all their colleagues about it, which is of course problematic unless you want your treatments contaminated and your study invalidated.

As long as we are overgeneralizing and creating caricatures, in their most obnoxious extreme we can depict the too helpful individual as something of a busybody, seeking control and authority over others, liking to identify with and agree with authorities, and often ignoring personal details in order to meddle in the details of others.

A subtype includes individuals who harbor a secret agenda and view your research as an opportunity to "do their own thing." In their classes they may add on to your project or even replace parts of it with their own ideas, which you may or may not find out about.

Another subtype consists of individuals who always have better ideas. An important subset of this type are thoughtful, practical teachers who see that your research isn't working well for some of their children and, because they want it to work well for all children, modify the treatment to make it work. If they are in your control conditions, you potentially face the unpleasant shock of finding out that the control students are showing impressive growth. At best, you are saddled with problems, because the intervention likely will have changed appreciably from what it conceptually was supposed to be. (We will return to this particular problem in a later chapter discussing implementation.) Others within this subtype we view less positively, for they may have inaccurate and naive views about what research is and how theories work, which makes any attempts of theirs to improve what you are doing produce opposite effects or introduce random noise to your data.

The too helpful staff person will certainly try your patience and pose a dilemma for you, particularly in the first and third variants. As the school environment is not one over which we have any authority, our strategies in coping with this type of individual are limited. As a first try, we could attempt to explain more fully what our goals are and why fidelity of treatment (viz., keeping the manipulations consistent with the ways the theoretical variables are supposed to be operationalized; accuracy of and consistency within each treatment condition) is so important. We could let the would-be helpers know that we are never too busy to worry about details, that because we are responsible for the project we need to be making the decisions, and that we don't want to burden them with work that should be done by us. If that doesn't work, we can try to find roles for them that take advantage of their enthusiasm (and desire for control) by giving them tasks that don't disrupt the project but that are important and useful (e.g., coordinating data collection or collecting staff reactions to the project). After all, these types of individuals have positive motives and, given some direction, they may put forth efforts that researchers can channel productively and draw upon for support. As a last resort, impose a rigid structure that specifies in detail what everyone is to do in any circumstance. One of the best ways (if not a necessary way) to assure that the treatments are being implemented correctly is to develop a careful implementation checklist to give to participants.

Overburdened

The overburdened staff member is a very different creature from all the others. This individual has a simple, straightforward response to your requests: "Sorry, but I am too busy to add anything else to my schedule." Such individuals often seem really to have trouble keeping up with the regular routines and may appear to struggle mightily to maintain equilibrium; it is not likely to do any good to show them that they really are doing no more than others who are coping. They may simply be lazy and will do almost anything to avoid any work, regularly assigned or otherwise, responding to additional work by avoiding it if possible; if they are told by their superiors that they have to participate, they will attempt to negotiate for release time elsewhere or turn passive-aggressive (see the next section). They are probably not ideal participants in your project. If they do participate, don't expect them to get all the details right, for their goal will be to cut as many corners as possible.

This type is a perfect one for illustrating the value of incentives. Providing them with replacement instruction, staff development time, additional class aides, and the like can help to change the routine that overwhelms them and foster enthusiasm in them for participating in your project. But chronic fatigue or laziness are not going to be remedied by small incentives. It can be a good idea to check out these individuals with the principal or some other staff to determine whether the individual is *always* overburdened or only expresses this complaint in connection with your project. Finally, there may be some instances in which the best decision is to exclude certain individuals from your study, for their participation may be guaranteed to be half-hearted and poorly organized.

Concrete Thinker

The "Concrete Thinker" is the type of individual who wants little authority and views order and preparation as ways of creating sanity among chaos. For such persons, a free-flowing discussion may be a nightmare, for in it they lose control of their classroom. Such individuals are typically pleasant and receptive to new ideas, but confused by them. As noted earlier, in an academic community we typically hold the expectation that individuals are used to and capable of mentally following the main ideas of oral presentations, and that they will ask questions if they are confused. Outside academia, however, expectations change. We have encountered individuals who don't follow oral presentations very well, who need concrete examples and illustrations in order to understand abstract ideas (some seem to encode issues in the concrete illustrations rather than the underlying principles), and who may be timid about speaking up when they are confused. Such individuals may hide their confusion, nodding as if agreeing with you and saying little in group settings. Later they will want all the details spelled out and will want to call you regularly for explanations and clarification. They will be difficult to identify, for their outward appearance and behaviors will be like those of their colleagues who understand what you are trying to explain. Only after experiencing frustration over their inability to implement your instructions might you realize that they do not understand the basic ideas and you need to get them openly to discuss their confusion.

Concrete thinkers are problems because they need extra help and guidance. In our experience, if you must have them participate, then you have little choice but to allocate additional time to assure that their behaviors will be consistent with those of their colleagues. They can consume much of your time with questions about small details and can inadvertently undermine your research by their inattentiveness to the big picture. But they can also help you to discover flaws in the precise ways that you set up your research, for they will take great pains to be sure that the details are correctly specified and are less willing to "wing it" to cover omissions or vagueness in your interventions. On balance, however, the concrete thinker type requires much more additional time than their attention to specifics and details gives back to you. Furthermore, if you fail to identify them before beginning the intervention, you are risking the loss of all data with which they are involved, for if they don't grasp the intricacies of your research, their attempts to implement your interventions likely will be imprecise.

Passive Resister

"Passive resisters" might alternatively be labeled "passive-aggressive." Such staff members may display hostile nonverbal behaviors, will be inattentive and may enjoy letting others around them know that they are bored, as by raising their eyebrows and rolling their eyes, and will at every opportunity do their best to undermine your research. They seem capable of mimicking behaviors their students use to harass them. They typically will not confront you directly, but will use places like the teachers' lounge to voice their dissatisfaction with and skepticism about your research. They will work to undermine staff morale.

A subset of this group is even less overt. They not only may not display any nonverbal behaviors to you, they may even hide their dissatisfaction from their peers. In such instances, their negative attitudes are reflected in subtle misbehaviors, for example forgetting to collect measures at the appropriate time or not giving students the correct amount of time on a timed task. Their mistakes may make them look like the concrete thinkers, but those mistakes are not accidental.

Passive resisters are difficult to deal with because you need first to identify them and then locate the sources of their hostility or antagonism before you can effectively confront it. Once you identify the problem, you need to determine the best way to confront it directly (publicly vs. individually) and whether you need to include in the discussions authority figures from the school. If the individual stays true to a passive response to confrontation, expect them to deny your assertions. Once the issue is broached directly, however, the behavior can much less easily be defended as inadvertent.

Crusty Veteran

> I think there are still a few people that I personally feel aren't willing to change or aren't willing to learn any more about it. I get the sense from them that they know as much as they need to know; and they've been teaching for so long that there really can't be anything that new. . . . You can sit and argue for hours and hours about people's beliefs and philosophies and get nowhere. (A teacher quoted in Wahlstrom, 1990, p. 280)

The remark above captures the essence of the "Crusty Veteran." That individual may be your typical closed book, the "don't bother me with the facts, my mind's already made up" type. After all, what has really changed in their classes over the past 25 or so years? Often, all too little. Since they use age as well as experience among their criteria for expertise, the younger the age of the researchers, the bigger the gap that will have to be bridged. Unfortunately, these types often have endless anecdotes about similar research projects from bygone times, and as they may be the only ones old enough to remember such projects, it is difficult to contradict their recollections. By virtue of their age they may have gained respect from their colleagues; after all, not everyone can survive for 20-odd years as a classroom teacher. They may attempt to take a senior spokesperson role and act as a lightning rod for other malcontents. Finally, one of the skills that may mark such senior spokespersons is that they don't need to outthink or outargue you; they can always fall back on the ol' country boy (or girl) routine with its folksy ways and incontrovertible conclusions. It's the old simple shtick, prefaced by some inane clause like "In my day . . . "

Once again, you have found a type of person to work around. Most important, you need allies to keep the climate positive and the enthusiasm going. People have to speak up against the crusty veterans; ideally, there will be other veterans who feel differently and can put their disruptive colleagues in their place. Crusty veterans need to be neutralized and their negative effects on staff morale and commitment minimized. Co-opting them remains a possibility, but it is probably not very likely, so you should plan on ways of responding directly to this type of individual. As their arguments are typically at the level of personal anecdotes, you might come prepared with some anecdotes of your own that speak to the value of your research. Best might be if you could point to

people from previous studies who at the beginning of the study expressed ideas similar to those of the crusty veteran, but after the study,
came up to you and said that they were wrong and your ideas really changed
the way they thought about schooling and the value of research.

Finally, for both the crusty veteran and the passive resister the risks
of confrontation need to be mentioned. If they are sufficiently confron-
tational or powerful, other staff members may back off in their support
of you and your project. After all, you are the outsider, and a choice
between supporting an outsider versus supporting a colleague is generally
an easy one to make.

Putting Them All Together

We have sketched in oversimplified and somewhat stereotypic ways
some of the common types of teachers and other school staff who might
confront you or disrupt your school-based research. The types are
diverse and the problems they bring complex, particularly when you
realize that a single individual may embody a number of different
problem types simultaneously. Even though we suggested potential
ways of dealing with each type, most important for neophyte researchers is a little prestudy paranoia about having the misfortune of meeting
all of the problem types in a single study. That paranoia should help you
to prepare for almost any problem, which should help smooth the path
you have to follow. In some instances, there may be politically feasible
solutions that allow all parties to maintain face while you get your study
conducted. As a last resort you could allow problem teachers to act as
if they are participating and implement whatever they feel like implementing. In such instances, minimize the time and resources directed
toward them, and be pleasant and supportive. At the same time, be sure
to identify them and their students in your data set and exclude their
data from your analyses. If you are particularly curious, you might
compare their class(es) with the others to see how their progress com-
pares with progress in your treatment and control conditions.

In concluding this chapter, we will attempt to back away from our
egocentric perspective and consider factors that could make even the
most dedicated teachers skeptical of research and researchers. First,
teachers typically don't see themselves as being hired to do research
and often feel as much the subject of research as the children in their
classes. Such feelings are likely compounded by the well-known body
of research that has involved deception of teachers (see, e.g., Rosenthal

& Jacobson, 1968). After all, if your research project really was attempting to study them unobtrusively, would you tell them the truth? (The answer for researchers to give is that given current requirements for informed consent we would need to tell them, but any apprehension they feel may be difficult to eliminate.) Second, all too many studies neglect the participants once the data are collected; many of us have been guilty of not providing timely and thorough feedback to schools about the results of our and their efforts. Third, teachers probably have heard but few instances where teachers actually gained anything from research studies; in fact, the presence of an outside expert who is capable of critically judging the quality of their teaching could increase their apprehensiveness and lead to worry about a negative evaluation being passed on to their superiors. As many schools provide very little feedback to teachers, a single instance of negative feedback can be extremely damaging. If you put yourself in the teacher's shoes, you might well find that you would view educational research as an opportunity to lose much but gain little.

A second set of issues centers on definitions of expertise and competence. Many teachers do what they do very well, and in fact might do less well if they were forced to use different approaches, particularly once the experts have made their exit from the scene. Is it in fact fair to ask teachers to use approaches with which they are uncomfortable or in which they don't believe? Are we making them more competent if we force them to change their approach to teaching? Would we personally want to have to employ a single approach to our teaching because some higher education researchers found that approach to be "better"? Such questions get to the heart of the teacher-researcher relationship and point to some major differences in purposes and desired ends.

A third set of issues will be discussed in more detail in a later chapter on implementation. Those issues focus on inherent conflicts between conceptually pure research and practically effective research. Virtually no educational research explains all of the variability in performance or affects the behavior of all students in the same way. Yet maintaining fidelity of treatment requires continuing with the intervention until the end of the study period. Although it is good research practice to maintain fidelity, how long can a teacher ethically go on when he or she sees that some subgroup of the students simply are not being served by the intervention? Increasing the magnitude of the problem is the criticism that most educational research is of short duration, whereas effectiveness of any intervention really requires extending it for a long enough period that spurious effects have time to diminish.

To summarize, there are some important reasons why teachers are skeptical of and cynical about research. As a researcher, one of your most important goals is to win the trust of school personnel so that your work goes smoothly. We hope that in this chapter we have helped you to consider issues and take perspectives that will help you to work more effectively with the people you might encounter in school settings.

EXERCISE

9. *Planning for School Audiences.* Imagine that you are preparing to conduct an intervention study that involves a number of classrooms. In the treatment conditions, students need to engage in strenuous physical activity for 5 minutes during each class period. Working in dyads, have one person role play a researcher presenting the project to school staff and the other the different teacher types. See how each type could disrupt your research. Sample queries might ask about girls in short skirts, physical contact between boys and girls, physically disabled students, and details about the treatment (when, what if time is short, etc.).

6

Selecting Measures: Comprehensiveness and Depth of Assessment Versus Brevity and Efficiency

This chapter examines the types of measurement issues that school researchers confront as they begin to collect data from children and staff in schools. We focus particularly on intervention studies, for those studies face extra demands related to measurement, namely, the need to collect measures that document the processes that occurred during the intervention. Consistent with our approach in the preceding chapters, our goal is not to repeat basic information that is given in standard texts (in the present case, measurement texts). We begin, however, with two basic measurement issues.

First, throughout this chapter we use terminology that emphasizes the distinction between the conceptual/theoretical variables that guide thinking of researchers, which we call "variables" or "constructs," and the observed variables that operationalize them, which we call "measures" or "instruments." Second, as a review for readers we define "reliability" and "validity." *Reliability* refers to the accuracy and consistency of a measure in assessing whatever it measures, *validity,* to the extent to which a measure actually assesses what it is intended to measure. Reliability is assessed by looking at the consistency (a) of responses across the items that make up a measure, called internal consistency, and (b) of measures across occasions and possibly settings, called test-retest. Validity (construct validity) is assessed by looking at the strength of the relations of a measure with other measures of the same theoretical variable (convergent validity) as well as with measures of other variables with which it should (convergent validity) and should not (discriminant validity) be related. Note that whereas assessing consistency requires only the measure of interest, validity cannot be assessed unless measures of other variables also are collected.

We assume that readers have some familiarity with basic issues of measurement and focus here on providing help in thinking about how those issues can and should be applied to school settings. We begin with a discussion of the types of measures that are commonly
collected in school settings. Then we consider how one goes about selecting measures that are appropriate, yet do not exceed either the reasonable attention span of students or a reasonable intrusion on class or staff time. We conclude the chapter by touching on a number of related issues, including (a) how developmental changes in students as they grow older can affect both measure selection and measure reliability, (b) accessing and using school file data, (c) existing large-scale data sets available for analyses, (d) the importance of collecting multiple measures of the constructs of interest, and (e) issues of standardization and scales of measures.

TYPES OF MEASURES COLLECTED IN SCHOOLS

This section provides an overview of some of the types of measures that are commonly collected by researchers working in educational settings. The types include information collected from both staff and students, and assessment that is indirect as well as direct. We pay special attention to intervention studies, for such studies require measures that can document that the intervention worked as planned.

We begin with the most common measures, those that tap student outcomes of schooling. Student outcomes encompass a wide range of student behaviors and attitudes, and may include dimensions like social relations, enjoyment of school, and motivation as well as more traditional categories like educational performance and problem-solving skills. Most measures can be obtained through direct assessment of the students by research staff. An alternative, indirect measure is for teachers to report on or appraise the students based on their observations of the students and their behaviors. A third method is to place trained observers in the classrooms to evaluate students. There is thus a broad array of measures that could be collected to assess student outcomes of schooling and a number of different ways of assessing those outcomes. As an aside, it is safer when collecting data to select widely used and well-validated instruments, for any deviations from generally accepted practice need to be accompanied by information fully documenting the reliability and validity of the measures used.

A second broad category of measures is process measures. Such measures assess what is happening during the time that the study is being conducted. Process measures could include amount of class participation, patterns of social interaction among students, leadership behaviors displayed, or time engaged working on the task. Many of these measures can assess both outcomes and process. For example, time spent engaged in learning could be an outcome measure if the purpose of a study is to increase engaged time, although it would be a process measure if engaged time is viewed as incidental to or not necessarily affected by the manipulation. Process measures are particularly important for intervention studies, for the outcomes of such studies typically are tied both to specifics of the manipulations and to a number of variables that may exist and vary within the setting where the research is conducted. In intervention studies, you need to determine whether the model is being implemented as intended and what is the relation of implementation to outcomes. If, for example, we were hypothesizing that school outcomes would improve if children were allowed to work in cooperative groups, we would want to collect measures that documented whether the cooperative groups were performing as we predicted they would. Such information logically could include students reporting on the behaviors of both themselves and their peers, teachers reporting on what they saw and heard, trained observers noting what they saw, and additional student measures such as unsolicited requests for more exercises using the intervention techniques or student attitudes about and liking for such techniques.

A third category of measures consists of measures that assess general teacher reactions to the research. In contrast to earlier measures that assessed teachers' evaluations of the behaviors of their students, these measures reflect teacher judgments about the measures, treatments, and interventions, and their reactions to them. Such reactions could include their immediate evaluations of and attitudes about the research, but also might include indirect measures, such as whether they use similar approaches in the weeks following the intervention (compared, potentially, to a baseline of their use prior to the intervention) or whether they plan to use such approaches. Additional useful information can also be gained from giving teachers a later opportunity to reflect upon and once again evaluate the project, including suggestions about what they see as its strengths and weaknesses. As for the preceding category of measures, these measures are particularly important for intervention studies.

Finally, if a researcher is interested in examining the more general impact of a study, then it is worthwhile to look for broad indices of its effects. For example, one might try to get parent reactions to a study by asking if their children talked about the research or whether children's patterns of studying at home changed during or after the study. Clearly, such measures are *very* indirect in measuring effects of research and are not likely to show much. Nonetheless, if you believe that the work you are doing will transform the classroom and the children, you should find ways of assessing the broad consequences of your research.

SELECTING MEASURES TO ADMINISTER IN SCHOOL SETTINGS

As researchers, we probably develop grand ideas about how school processes operate, and we may believe in those ideas strongly enough to want to collect measures of all of the variables that interest us. If we are like many of our colleagues, we may be tempted to throw into the mix extra measures that seem to be related to just about everything. These make for peace of mind during instances when we ask ourselves "What do we do if nothing in our study works?" The best variables of this type are ones that take little or no effort to collect. One classic variable of this type is birth order, which for a variety of reasons, including spuriousness, has been found stastically to be significantly related to everything from achievement to attainment to social skills (see, e.g., Miller & Maruyama, 1975; Schooler, 1972). Including such variables may turn out to be informative, but their inclusion can draw the focus away from what is more important. Research needs to balance (often atheoretical) data exploration ("fishing") with conceptually grounded investigation (theory testing).

Unfortunately, once we make sure that we have multiple measures of each variable and total up our list of measures, we are likely reaching the limits of student time (not to mention teacher tolerance) in the 175-day school year. As you develop your instruments, you must think seriously about how much class time you will be requesting and about student and teacher attention spans. We try in our own research to request as little class time for completing instruments as we can get by with, to send the message that we view class time as precious and that our goal is to disrupt learning minimally if at all. Incidentally, lack of sensitivity to this issue can even result in phone calls from the local teachers' union!

To illustrate our discussion, we will return to our study of low-achieving students, focusing first on measures for school staff and then on measures for children. As we noted earlier, the schools we considered for inclusion in our study were participating in a project called the Minnesota Educational Effectiveness Project (MEEP). That project focused on 15 characteristics that had been identified by educational research as being related to effective educational programs and effective schools (for a more complete description, see Maruyama et al., 1989). Because ongoing attempts at staff development were focused on those characteristics and we wanted to find schools with school climates that were fairly similar, we decided that we needed to assess those 15 characteristics. Unfortunately, however, there was no instrument available, which leads us to issues related to the development of measures.

Given the broad classification schemes used in defining the 15 characteristics we easily could have developed an instrument containing 150 or more items (i.e., 10 per characteristic). We quickly decided against such an instrument, because we needed to use our instrument twice each school year for 3 years. We felt that the enthusiasm of school staff for the instrument would quickly wane, both within and across administrations, and we wanted to minimize the kinds of responses made by bored respondents whose primary goal is to finish a questionnaire. We decided instead to attempt to develop three to four items per characteristic that would reasonably reflect each domain of interest, even if the intercorrelations among items was less than desired. Obviously, we could have maximized intrascale reliabilities even with short scales by restricting the items and narrowly defining each characteristic; such an approach, however, should show lesser validity despite having reasonably good reliability. (Our point is *not* that our way is the only way or perhaps even the "best" way, for low reliability creates problems. Some of our colleagues likely would look unfavorably at our approach, as it results in relatively low reliabilities. In schools, however, the trade-off between reliability and time spent testing forces difficult choices.)

Items were selected by a procedure that began with us developing items that reflected the most important aspects of each of the characteristics. We then went to the people who formed the statewide advisory committee for MEEP and asked them, first individually and then in small groups, to match each of the items we had developed with its characteristic. After discussion, we excluded items about which we and they disagreed and trimmed each scale down to no more than 4 items. Our final instrument consisted of 50 items. From our perspective, the process came out about as well as we could have expected, as it yielded an instrument with a reasonably small number of items and yet that seemed from both our perspective and that of the persons designing the MEEP to tap the intended dimensions. Because all the items had a common response format, we expected that school personnel would be able to complete the instrument in 30 minutes or less.

When we focused on assessment of students, time issues again were of major importance. Initially, we hoped that we would be able to manage by making use of existing schoolwide tests, but we found that differences both within and across sites made use of available data impractical (more on this in a later section of this chapter). We therefore needed to find an instrument for measuring educational progress. Further, that instrument would have to be relatively short (i.e., ideally take students no more than 30 minutes to complete), administrable in a group setting, and relatively simply scored (as we needed to give it to more than 3,500 students). We wanted it to cover reading, spelling, written expression, and math. Again, our desire for such a brief instrument was spurred by our need to administer the instrument at least twice each school year as well as our desire to collect additional information without presenting unrealistic demands for classroom time. We also needed an instrument that was common across sites so we would be able to judge comparability of the classification systems that the different schools used to assign students to special education programs.

After considering a number of standardized instruments, we again decided to develop our own, which we called the Basic Academic Skills Samples (BASS; see, e.g., Espin, Deno, Maruyama, & Cohen, 1989). After conducting initial instrument reliability and validity studies, we decided to go ahead and use the BASS; even though it had lesser reliability than longer, normed instruments that we considered as alternatives, it showed reasonable patterns of relations with them and showed good discrimination both across skill levels within grades and across grades. Notably, it is now used by a number of other projects that are also working with students with mild disabilities and thus provides a common, easily administered instrument for assessing impacts of those projects.

Finally, lest readers get the impression that, contrary to our earlier suggestion, our typical approach is to ignore available instruments and develop our own (with dangers of unreliability and invalidity), we should note that for measures of personality and competence we used only instruments that were widely used and normed for elementary students. These instruments were administered only once, which made us less concerned about time spent in administering them, but we used short forms of scales whenever possible.

These examples illustrate the complexity of finding measures that meet the criteria of reliability and validity yet that can easily be administered. All too often, we have found that instruments we initially think we want to use turn out to be much too long for use in schools, particularly with young children in elementary school. Researchers need to find ways to cut administration time without losing too much in the areas of reliability and validity. They need to ask themselves repeatedly whether all of the desired measures are necessary.

In our view, ancillary instruments are often not worth collecting, for using them can diminish participant willingness to complete the measures and can affect their attitudes about participation. Some researchers suggest adding the extra measures at the end of the testing session so they don't affect the responses to other items. That approach may not get around the problem, however, for participants likely want (and deserve) to know how long the session is and the amount of work remaining at various points in time. Negative effects are particularly likely if the measures are all stapled together in a single packet. Thus, those extra instruments add administration time and can alter participants' views about how reasonable you are being. Any adverse reactions to the time demands can appreciably affect the data, particularly when rating scales and self-report procedures are used.

RELIABILITY AND VALIDITY AT VARIOUS AGES

For researchers working with a range of ages, but particularly for work with elementary school populations, differential reliability and validity at different ages and changes in variability across age can create problems both in developing instruments and in analyzing them. For example, consider assessing math skills at various ages. An ideal instrument needs to demonstrate reasonable reliability and validity all across the elementary years. Thus, the measure has to be difficult enough to discriminate among the abilities of high-achieving sixth graders (i.e., avoid compression of scores at the upper end of the distribution, called ceiling effects) and yet be easy enough to discriminate among the skills of various primary grade children who have at best rudimentary math skills (i.e., avoid bottom-end compression, or floor effects).

At some ages finding reliable and valid tests may be impossible. For example, there may be little reason for assessing math skills in first grade, for many schools do not teach enough math skills to first graders for there to be much variability in the children's responses. If the skills are assessed by a pretest-posttest model, many of the individual pretest scores will likely be very close to zero (so much for having a normal distribution). Second, depending upon the skills that are taught at various ages, there may appear on tests to be ages at which children improve their abilities dramatically and others where they seem to learn little or nothing. Third, as children get older the distance between the highest- and lowest-scoring individuals increases and variance within single age groups increases, which causes problems if age is not taken into account. (This issue will be revisited in our discussion about standardization.) Fourth, if students of all ages are thrown together for analyses, two disruptive processes will be operating: (a) when linear relationships between variables that change monotonically (i.e., steadily increasing or decreasing) with age (e.g., correlating math achievement with reading achievement) are examined, the findings will be confounded with age because developmental effects will help produce or greatly strengthen those linear relationships; and (b) for comparisons of group means as well as of relationships between variables, assumptions about equal variances (homogeneity, homoscedasticity) likely will be violated.

Age of the sample may also be related to reliability of the measures used. Reliability typically will increase as the range of scores expands, so increases in reliability should be expected to accompany increases in age for many measures used across the elementary school years. At the same time, however, it is not uncommon for the number of dimensions tapped by an instrument to increase as children age, which can make changes in reliability much less predictable. What may begin as a unidimensional skill during the early elementary school years may branch out into two or more related yet distinct skills as children age; if we were to attempt to assess reliability still assuming that our measure taps only a single dimension, our reliability estimates would depend upon the strength of the relationship between the related but distinct skills. Thus, reliability for the older children could be higher or lower than reliability for younger children.

Validity issues may be even more complex than issues of reliability, for they depend upon patterns of relationships across as well as within constructs. If each of the measures of interest is changing across time (and ages of subjects) and the dimensionality of some of them is increasing, discerning patterns of construct validity will be complicated if not impossible. Assessing convergent and discriminant validity with any degree of accuracy requires an understanding of the constructs that underlie measures that are collected as well as what is happening to each across time. Without such knowledge, errors of inference are likely to be made.

Once again, unfortunately, we cannot prescribe a simple solution. The solution to any particular problem in this area requires understanding what is happening to the actual measure that is collected. Our purpose is instead to make readers consider the implications of changes due to development and growth on both the measures they plan to collect as well as the constructs that underlie those measures. Then they can try to anticipate both the nature of changes and the effects of those changes on their data. You need to develop an understanding of how the dimensionality underlying your measures changes for different age groups you sample. Such an understanding could be attained through background literature surveys, through pretesting, or even through preliminary data analyses once the data are collected. Ideally, however, one should know prior to using a measure whether or not it meets the needs of the research.

ACCESSING STUDENT FILE DATA

At some point in your investigation, you will undoubtedly be told about the school files. Files likely will seem promising, for they contain potentially interesting and useful data. Nonetheless, there are numerous disincentives for using file data. Most prominent among these are privacy regulations and noncomparability across classes, grades, and schools.

First, consider access. In many schools, only school personnel are allowed to look at school files (sometimes called cumulative files). The reasoning is sound; no one wants individuals snooping around the file information to see what they can find. The teacher expectation research (see, e.g., Rosenthal & Jacobson, 1968) illustrates potential dangers that may result from giving teachers access to expectancy-shaping information. Even though there are fewer possible adverse consequences of researchers having access to expectancy-shaping information, school personnel nevertheless may feel uncomfortable about letting you look directly at the files, for you may see information beyond that which you are authorized to use and you may inadvertently "mess up" the files. One solution is to have a school staff member get the information for you, which may require you to reimburse the school for the individual's time and also makes you dependent upon the vagaries of that person's schedule. You are not likely to be seen as the most important part of that person's job.

A second issue of major importance is that because children are minors, they cannot personally release their file information; either school district or parental consent or both are needed. Thus, any request to access file information likely needs to go through the same informed-consent procedures that are required for new data that you collect.

Even if permission to use file information is granted, there may be certain types of information that will be protected. For example, some districts will not allow information about ethnicity or racial background to be released without special permission from the school district central office. Even if your request for access is approved, you will likely be amazed at how imprecisely and nonuniformly the data are compiled and how much information is missing. Students who transfer from other districts will at best have different types of information in their files and are likely to have no data at all from other districts in which they attended schools. (We should note that virtually no resources are available to schools for organizing and maintaining student files.)

Even more discouraging are problems in using available data. As an example, imagine that we decide to use available data on standardized achievement tests. It is not unusual in a project like ours, involving 12 schools, to be confronted with 12 different patterns of achievement testing, one for each school. Different schools use different tests and change the tests they use both across grades and over time. They also may test the different grades at different points during the school year. Some schools decide to skip administering standardized tests to particular grades, focusing their attention, for example, on testing at grades 1, 3, and 5.

Changing tests across grades seems eminently reasonable to school personnel; they do not want to administer the same instrument repeatedly to children year after year. By changing tests, they will not have to worry about factors like test-specific learning that could improve performance upon retesting. Changing tests across grades also lets children whose performance is adversely impacted by idiosyncracies of a particular test to build a broader profile of test performance across time. If test expense is an important issue, money can be saved if tests are given every other year rather than every year or if less expensive tests are used some years or in certain grades. Communities and school boards can also be fiercely independent about their curriculum and thus unwilling to be part of any attempt to collect common data across district lines.

Given the above dynamics of standardized tests, school-file achievement data are generally inadequate for researchers who attempt to do research with a cross-grade and cross-school sample. There is the possibility of converting each of the test scores to a common scale of measurement, for example, to its grade equivalent or to its normal curve equivalent, and then pooling scores across tests. In such instances, however, potential noncomparability of different tests makes using them as the primary measures of performance very risky. Furthermore, inconsistencies between sites in where and how tests are administered will produce problems; once we add into the equation the facts that children are tested at different points in the school year and that different districts test different grades, we have a problem that even sophisticated methodologists wish to avoid (without even considering missing data).

If you decide that you want to use standardized test data, the best of all worlds would be a situation where your study is small enough that all of your subjects have the same test data available. If not, your best alternative would be to convince all the schools with which you are working to use the same test and to administer it to all grades at approximately the same time in the school year. If they refuse, you could yourself administer the test that you like best to all students (with consequent high costs).

Alternatively, imagine that you decide only to use file data to supplement other data that are to be collected. Even then the disincentives may be too great. Even though standardized test scores from file data may well provide useful supplementary information, they are costly to collect (they require additional permissions, staff time, and still yield incomplete data). Thus, they may prove to be impractical even for such limited uses.

Once again, our intent is not to get you to give up before you start or to convince you to reject the idea of using file data, but to help you recognize the potential difficulties you are likely to encounter when accessing such data. Actually, we each have persisted and used file data (e.g., standardized test scores, classification information for special education services) as part of research projects we have done in schools. Those data, however, were never as easy and available as they seemed upon first (superficial) examination. Such data obviously are easiest to use if you work only with students from a single grade within a single school.

EXISTING DATA SETS

For some types of educational research, existing large scale data sets provide an important resource. Even though they may reward "niche seeking" (i.e., finding small but heretofore unexplored problem areas), they also allow researchers to think about measurement issues and to begin to address scoring issues without actually collecting data. Probably most prominent among these data sets is the National Assessment of Educational Progress (NAEP), which assesses the educational achievement of U.S. schoolchildren on a regular basis. NAEP data include variables on educational performance. Other widely used data sets include broad longitudinal surveys like High School and Beyond, or Youth in Transition.

Access to data sets such as the NAEP is relatively simple; NAEP data even can be obtained through meetings of the American Educational Research Association. Access to the other data sets, which are collected by funded researchers, is somewhat different but still not difficult. For individuals situated on major research campuses, access typically is coordinated through interuniversity research consortiums and cooperative arrangements among universities. There are costs for these data, which are typically in the form of a data tape or disks, accompanied by a manual providing documentation for the information. If you are interested in a particular data set and are uncertain whether it is available for secondary analyses, the best bet probably is to contact the original researchers, particularly one of the principal investigators. Such individuals would know not only whether the data are available but also how to access them if they are available.

Once again, however, such data often are less attractive than they first may appear to be. Many of the large-scale data sets were created to answer policy questions rather than theoretical questions, with the result that much of the available data are neither very useful nor very interesting for purposes of theory testing or development. The level of aggregation of the data can also make them less relevant for problem solving at the school or class level.

COLLECTING MULTIPLE MEASURES OF VARIABLES OF INTEREST

One of the major shortcomings experienced by individuals who attempt to do secondary analyses of data sets collected by others is the likelihood of sparseness of measures on the variables of greatest interest to them. Most likely if the relations that interest the secondary researcher were also those of greatest interest to the primary researcher, not only would the variables be assessed in more depth, but research questions about those issues almost certainly would have been addressed by the primary researcher. Measures that from the perspective of the primary researcher were less central would be measured less intensively.

Other factors can contribute to a shortage of measures. First, can be a "cohort" problem insofar as the fairly recent emergence of techniques like latent variable structural equation modeling has increased the need for multiple measures (see, e.g., Jöreskog & Sörbom, 1989; Maruyama & McGarvey, 1980). That is, because many of the data sets available for secondary analyses provide data collected a number of years ago when there were fewer reasons to collect multiple measures of each variable of interest, those studies often do not contain multiple measures for many of their variables. Additional factors are (a) pressures to minimize use of class time in educational research, which has led researchers to collect only single measures of many variables of interest to them, and (b) the use of research to direct policy, which puts a much lower priority on collecting multiple measures of theoretical variables.

Before addressing the complications caused by trying to minimize intrusiveness of assessment on class time and student learning, we will try to explain why multiple measures are needed. The availability of multiple measures is critically important for addressing issues of construct validity and of reliability. For this discussion, reliability is defined solely in terms of a measure's accuracy in tapping the underlying theoretical variable or construct. More commonly, reliability includes all sources of internal consistency of items, including common sources of variance due to methods as well as the underlying construct. Thus, an upper bound for reliability with respect to the underlying theoretical variable is provided by internal consistency reliability; its estimate of reliability includes stable variance from the underlying construct of interest, from common methods, and from any other sources of common variance. It reflects consistency of the measure or instrument used rather than how accurately that measure assesses the conceptual variable that underlies it.

Consider as an example a measure of a child's family social class. Family social class can be assessed by different measures, including family educational attainment, family occupational status, and family income. Each of these could potentially be measured with perfect accuracy (and, by a traditional definition, with perfect reliability), yet, because each measure imperfectly assesses social class, research findings could change dramatically depending upon which measure is used in a particular study. If we decide to measure social class by a single measure, which do we pick? How about using a composite measure? Even in this case, each part of the composite is flawed regardless of the accuracy of coding of individual responses, so a simple summing of the items leaves an imprecise variable. For example, a measure of educational attainment, even if perfectly reliable from a perspective of traditional reliability, typically ignores where the education is from, counting a degree from Harvard or Princeton just like a mail-order degree of the same nominal level. Thus, degrees are at best an imprecise measure of the underlying variable of family social class. Only if additional measures of family social class are collected would assessment of the imprecision inherent in that measure be possible.

The advantage of multiple measures is that they allow us to estimate the common variance component across the measures and determine more accurately the extent to which we are measuring what we want to measure (see, e.g., Costner & Schoenberg, 1973; Kenny, 1979). In addition, the availability of multiple measures aids in the estimation of construct validity, for it provides a pattern of relationships (rather than a single relationship) across each pair of conceptual variables. The available information can be used to assess covariation of the conceptual variables of interest more adequately (see Costner & Schoenberg, 1973). Judging convergent and discriminant validity becomes more precise when multiple measures of each construct are available.

The combined pressures to use minimal class time and to collect multiple measures of each variable create major problems, but these can be minimized by using concise instruments and by devising multiple ways to operationalize variables. For example, in some instances, single questions that ask directly about the variable of interest can provide important information that complements a widely used scale. If we were interested in assessing students' general self-concept, in addition to a standard self-concept scale we could both ask teachers about each child's general feelings of self-worth and ask individual children directly about their self-image. Not only do we then have data that operationalize self-concept in differing ways, but we also have kept our data collection fairly brief.

In short, there are alternatives to collecting for each dimension of interest three long and widely used scales. The challenges will undoubtedly make you think creatively, but collecting multiple measures is important and worth attempting.

SCALING AND STANDARDIZATION

Some of the more complex issues that we attempt to address in this book are those related to scaling and standardization. They are not issues that we have found easy to present, because they require statistical and methodological skills in excess of those required for most of the rest of this book (for additional information, see DeVellis, 1990). We will begin this section by speaking generally about issues of scale or metric. Then we will try to give more practical suggestions about how you might attempt to make data compatible for analyses across grades.

Researchers frequently present standardized relationships because standardized scores (z-scores, etc.) and relationships (correlations, standardized regression coefficients) are scaled in an intuitively straightforward way that facilitates their interpretation. Within single samples, such an approach is fine. If, however, a researcher wants to make comparisons across subgroups or from one population to another, any comparisons need to be done using nonstandardized coefficients, for only those coefficients maintain the unique and potentially differing metric or scale of each of the groups.

For example, consider our study of low-achieving children. Assume that we collect data only from those children. Because any achievement variables include only part of the whole distribution of possible scores, their range is restricted. Any attempts to examine the relations of achievement variables with other variables come up against problems caused by the restriction of range; as the standard deviation of the achievement scores is limited, correlations of achievement with other variables will be reduced. The (unstandardized) covariance of achievement scores with other variables should not be affected, however. For example, if we were to look at the raw score relationship of achievement and teacher ratings, we might find that, in each of two samples, every 5-point increase in achievement scores was accompanied by a 2-point increase in teachers' ratings of intellectual skills. For the two samples, the covariance would be the same across the samples, but the correlation would be smaller in the sample with restricted range (and smaller standard deviation).

The point is that it is correct to compare the magnitude of correlations across populations or studies only if the standard deviations for each variable are the same in the two populations or studies—in other words, it is almost never appropriate to compare correlations. For example, numerous studies have compared correlations found in male samples with correlations found in female samples, ignoring whether or not the standard deviations of variables in the respective samples were the same. A second point worth noting is that just because other investigators find significant correlations and you do not may not mean that your findings are different from theirs. Your standard deviations may just be smaller, and your correlations therefore smaller as well.

We now turn from issues of standardization for data analyses to issues of scaling in conducting analyses of a multigrade sample. As we noted earlier, such analyses are complicated by developmental changes and increases in variability as children grow older. Perhaps the best approach is as much as possible to conduct analyses within grade; such analyses avoid both of the above problems. If, however, analyses of multigrade samples are needed, other options need to be considered. One possibility would be selecting ways to transform scores that more strongly affect the grades that have larger variability (such as square root or log transformations). A weakness of transformed scores is that the links of the scores to the items that generated them become obscured. Further, means of scores following nonlinear transformations like square root or log transformations are more difficult to interpret.

Speaking generally, your choices depend on the analyses that need to be done. For example, if we want to compare growth rates across grades, one alternative to raw score growth would be to use the pretest means and standard deviations for each grade as a baseline and to measure growth from each baseline. Practically, that can be done by scaling each student's posttest score in terms of the pretest mean and standard deviation from all students in that student's grade, namely, by subtracting each individual's score from the pretest mean and then dividing that difference score by the standard deviation.

If you instead undertake correlational analyses, you might consider standardizing scores within grade before doing the analyses, for that removes the effects of grade from the analyses. In effect you overlay each grade upon each other grade, taking away any mean differences and any differences in variability across grades.

Finally, we consider scaling issues as they relate to ways of presenting data so they will be meaningful to school personnel. For example, in some of our analyses, we have arbitrarily scaled student scores within each grade to provide a mean of 100 and a standard deviation of 15. We chose that particular metric to present the scores because it is familiar to educators from exposure to intelligence and other tests that are scaled to a similar metric. To make scores interpretable, logical approaches to scaling issues need to be complemented by strategies that facilitate ease of interpretation. For example, visual displays are usually readily interpretable, particularly widely used and relatively well-understood figures like graphs, pie diagrams, and histograms (e.g., Figure 9.1).

This short overview of scaling should help you think about the problems and complexities of selecting appropriate scales both for reporting findings and for conducting analyses. Unfortunately, many problems of scaling are quite complex, precluding our providing broad solutions. We hope our thoughts and suggestions will help readers to anticipate potential problems that they might encounter as well as to consider the consequences of various alternative approaches that could be tried.

EXERCISE

10. *Standardized Tests.* Find a copy of a manual for a standardized test. How does it address age differences? Are there recommendations for working simultaneously with different age groups? Are there grade-equivalent scores, normal curve equivalents, and/or other normed scores? Would you use this test repeatedly with the same sample? Are the tests for different ages very different? How expensive is the test to use? If you needed to save money, how high a priority would use of tests like this one be to you?

7

How Long Does My Study Need to Last?

In this chapter we turn in detail to questions of time, examining a number of issues related to duration of any study that is being planned. For research designed to have an impact on school practices, particularly educational techniques, the issues discussed here should be central ones, but for research that has as its purpose to collect single-wave data about information like student attitudes or behaviors, this chapter may not be particularly relevant. Such research may well take participants only one sitting, will at most be short term, and does not attempt to suggest changes in educational strategies or approaches.

The issues covered in this chapter include (a) should time be spent collecting pretest data, that is, is the study intended to measure changes or only posttest differences (a return to the design issues presented earlier); (b) how long does the intervention need to be; (c) should there be long-term follow-up of the findings; and (d) should consideration of issues surrounding types of school restructuring be included as part of study preparation.

CHANGE VERSUS POSTSTUDY DIFFERENCE

In Chapter 4 we discussed experimental, quasi-experimental, and nonexperimental designs. At that time we did not, however, focus explicitly on how design is affected by the need for and importance of assessing change. Even though the decision to collect pretest measures is one that should be widely understood, as it is basic to design issues, we will begin with it here.

If the research is truly experimental—which should mean that it includes random assignment of subjects to conditions—then pretests are not needed, for the assumption is made that random assignment of subjects to conditions produces equivalence of groups. Generally, control through random assignment is sufficient; in fact, collecting pretest data is risky since pretest differences are often difficult to interpret in meaningful ways. It is important to remember that regardless of the probability level that is established for minimizing Type I error (i.e., the likelihood of wrongly rejecting the null hypothesis) in research, chance differences between groups will occur occasionally (at .05, or 5 times in 100). Chance differences, then, may appear on pretest scores even with random assignment. The possibility of finding significant pretest differences raises the question of how many such differences can or should be ignored as being "noise," rather than substantive. (As an aside, because subject responses across measures are typically not independent of one another, it should not be surprising to find that groups differ on a number of measures once group differences are found on one measure. To control for covariation between measures and for chance findings when multiple measures are collected, the appropriate level for assessing whether differences exceed conventional levels of statistical significance is the study rather than the individual measures. Thus, multivariate tests that yield a study-level significance test are appropriate.) Rather than attempting to provide a simple answer to a complex question in an area about which we are not particularly expert, we instead suggest that the array of research design and methods texts be used as resources to provide guidance here (e.g., Judd et al., 1990).

Just as preexisting differences are easily misinterpreted, the absence of significant differences on pretest measures also is not particularly revealing. Finding that pretest scores do not differ significantly across groups confirms only what was expected: that the assignment of subjects to conditions appears in fact to be random on the variables of interest. It does not guarantee, however, that groups actually are equivalent on those variables, for the test looks for significant differences rather than equality of means across conditions; means can differ quite a bit without being significantly different. Imprecision of measurement due to unreliability or invalidity of tests can also mask true differences.

Imagine that you conduct pretesting and find between-group differences. Now you know more than you would have known if you had not gathered pretest data, but you may also know too much, for you know that there is an alternative explanation for any poststudy, between-condition differences that you find, without knowing the relative contributions of the two sources (the treatment and the pretest differences) of difference. Also, as the groups started at different points on the pretest, an interaction of treatment by pretest level is also possible. For example, an intervention that works better with students who are below some threshold level would work very differently if most students began the study below that threshold than if most began above it. Thus, pretest differences could obscure or even reverse the effectiveness of an intervention. The point is not that pretesting should be avoided, for there is value in discovering that your groups were not equivalently divided. Rather, the point is that design issues should drive your decisions on how and when to collect data. If you feel uncertain about the effectiveness of your random assignment on variables of interest, you likely will be better off checking on the randomness and if necessary redividing participants before beginning your study.

In practice, there likely will be few situations in which clear patterns of significant pretest differences emerge and also few in which the groups are exactly equivalent on the dimensions of interest. Instead, in most circumstances there will be small differences between groups that may be just large enough to be bothersome and make you consider somehow trying to control for pretest scores, which really is not the suggested approach for experimental designs.

Finally—and very important for project efficiency and the effective use of school time—there is every reason not to spend time collecting (unnecessary) pretest data for experimental studies. Not only do the additional measures require extra class time, but potential sensitizing effects of pretesting can emerge. If systematic examination of the effects of pretesting is done, the design is made more complicated and, potentially, the necessary sample size is increased. In short, we see little to gain and time and effort wasted in pretesting when doing experimental research.

For research in school settings, however, the reality is that true experiments are difficult to conduct, especially if the study is to run over a long period of time. For example, in our study of low-achieving special education students, laws and regulations preclude random assignment of subjects to conditions. Thus, quasi-experimental and nonexperimental research methods are needed to judge the effectiveness of different programmatic approaches.

For quasi-experimental and nonexperimental research, the absence of random assignment suggests that taking into account pretest differences is a necessary part of any study. Analyses designed to take pretest differences into account attempt to adjust scores on poststudy measures to control for preexisting differences between groups. Such analyses can include analysis of raw score change or difference scores, repeated measures analyses, or analysis of adjusted difference scores using techniques like analysis of covariance. It is important to note, however, that such mathematical adjustments do not necessarily assure that comparisons are valid. Paralleling an earlier example, one might imagine instances in which students who score high on a pretest score are affected much more positively by an intervention than are their peers whose scores are poorer. Thus, if students from the experimental conditions scored much higher on a pretest than did the students in the control conditions, the effects of the treatment might look very positive even after controlling for pretest scores. If, however, the pattern of pretest differences on scores between the treatment and control conditions were reversed, the effects of the treatment might appear to be negative even after adjusting for pretest differences. Thus, pretest differences can be problematic insofar as they may reflect other pervasive differences between the groups that cannot be removed simply by adjusting posttest scores mathematically. On balance we recommend analyses that attempt to take out the influences of preexisting differences, but we make this recommendation reluctantly, for such approaches can lead to misinterpretations. Here again, there simply are no easy answers to complex problems.

HOW LONG DO INTERVENTIONS NEED TO LAST?

In this section we focus on research that attempts to evaluate some aspect of the school environment. How long does an educational intervention need to be to provide an adequate test of the effectiveness of that intervention?

To put the current discussion into context of a "real" educational issue, we will tie it to the literature on cooperative group learning and goal structures. The cooperative learning literature is filled with interventions that have lasted between a day and a week. Of particularly short duration are many of the studies conducted with college students; some of these are single occasion, or one-shot studies. Short-duration interventions have been criticized for a number of reasons, including (a) susceptibility to alternative phenomena such as "novelty" effects, that is, effects that occur with any new technique because of the novelty or differentness of the approach rather than the specifics of the technique; (b) the possibility of Hawthorne type effects (see Homans, 1965), in which the increased attention that accompanies implementation of an innovation increases participants' motivation; or (c) being too short to impact what really goes on in schools. Implicit in the criticisms is that results obtained from longer studies are more meaningful.

From our perspective, the criticisms raise an interesting and important point, namely that over time, as a body of research on a topic begins to accumulate, the research literature needs to stand the test of time and show that the initial findings will endure. It is important to know how interventions are likely to fare if they were to become a regular part of educational practice. In response to such requirements, modifications of the interventions will need to stretch them across longer time periods (as well as away from their original advocates and from the research community to the educational practice community) to see whether the initial impact of an intervention is sustainable over longer durations.

At the same time, however, to criticize or discount all studies of short duration seems to us to be too simplistic. The accumulation of scientific knowledge occurs as the result of a broad array of practical and conceptual replications and extensions. Such extensions and replications include varying the treatment across differing time periods. Furthermore, it hardly makes sense to design early research attempts in an area to last an entire school year or to design only modifications of initially promising approaches that require a semester or more to evaluate. Varying the length and intensity of interventions is important in the same manner as using both experimental and nonexperimental approaches or both quantitative and qualitative types of analyses in research: They provide greater opportunities for accumulation of knowledge and for convergence on more enduring conclusions. Studies of varying duration and intensity allow relatively quick analysis of the effects of variations of treatments, promote a better understanding of the importance of specific facets of the interventions (i.e., what makes a difference), and permit an evaluation of the impacts of time on various treatments. It is also important to distinguish between preliminary work and work on widely accepted principles. By the time treatments have become "standard educational practice," we would hope that some tests of those treatments would have been of long duration.

To put this discussion in context, let us return to the illustration of the cooperative group learning and goal structure studies. That literature contains studies ranging from a single hour to those stretching across entire school years. This array of different study durations has allowed researchers attempting to conduct syntheses of the literature to look at length of time as a variable in order to see whether duration of study seems to make a difference on the favorableness of the outcomes (e.g., Johnson, Maruyama, Johnson, Nelson, & Skon, 1981). In fact, in the cooperative learning literature, shorter studies have tended to report stronger findings, but as different investigators have conducted the various studies and have varied their methods on dimensions other than study duration, many alternative explanations exist for the differences in findings across studies. For the cooperative learning literature to date, one of the most important results of the diverse array of study durations has been that investigators have been directed toward systematically examining the effects of study duration. (Note that much can be done to look at the effects of study duration within long studies if measures are collected at varying points during the study.)

From a different perspective, we might raise the question whether time itself can ever be the central issue. To paraphrase a statement once made by a colleague of ours, "In research, time is an empty vessel." The problem is certainly much more complex than simply looking at duration of an intervention. For example, a cooperative goal structure study that coincides with a particular curriculum unit is certainly long enough to determine whether children learn that unit better under a cooperative goal than under alternative goal structures. In contrast, a study of how children learn how to read would be difficult to accomplish in so short a period. The effects of learning under differing goal structures is complicated immensely by what else goes on in the schools and classes that are being studied. With respect to the goal structuring literature, as far as we know no investigators argue for teaching using only a single-goal structure, which means that any long-term intervention will likely contain mixed goal structure elements. Thus, any long-term study will almost certainly end up comparing mixed structures with other potentially mixed but different structures, which may provide a test of effectiveness of cooperative goal structures, but may reflect a number of other factors as well.

Our point is that researchers need to think about what is most important in the body of literature on which they want to have an impact and attempt to determine the type of studies that are most needed. How one resolves an issue like duration of the study can vary greatly, depending upon the existing literature and the potential impact of the research on educational practice.

IS LONG-TERM FOLLOW-UP WORTHWHILE?

Imagine that you have completed your research, turned in the final report, talked to school staff about what you found, and even shepherded your work through the publication process to the point at which you see the light of day at the end. You're feeling good about the work and decide to go back to the school to visit your living legacy. What are you likely to find? Will the project still be ongoing, an institutionalized part of the school curriculum? Unfortunately, the answer will vary greatly from study to study, depending upon vagaries like whether the internal advocates stayed at the school and continued promoting the idea or whether another "hot" idea came along to replace yours. In any case, our goal here is to help you think about the issues that need to be confronted if you decide to go back and follow up on your research.

Consider the case in which you plan from the inception of your study to go back and collect long-term follow-up data. In that instance, you can advocate for long-term follow-up from the beginning. In such circumstances, the primary issues for you may be anticipating staff turnover and student attrition. Staff turnover is likely to be beyond your control, but can have a major impact on your long-term results. Imagine the worst case, with total turnover. In such an instance, the persons working with your strategies do not know you and learned about your approaches secondhand if at all. It would not be surprising to find that the intervention has changed in important ways (probably not to your liking) and you are again an outsider who has to build up the trust of school staff members as well as train them in how to implement the interventions. Thus, it is worthwhile, if you plan to gather long-term follow-up data, to do what you can to identify and work with staff members whose continued presence at your sites is most likely (or choose sites with relatively low staff turnover). In addition, it is worthwhile to get whatever future commitments you can from current staff.

Student attrition and problems that arise from nonrandom loss of subjects were discussed earlier. Of particular importance are (a) individual-level loss of lower-class and minority students, who tend to be more mobile (as renters) and thus overrepresented in the attrition group; and (b) program-level loss due to changes in school programs and in the students who choose them. An extreme case of this last problem is discussed later in this chapter.

In many instances your original plans may not have included any follow-up, but controversies about specific programs or discussions about converting research into practice could lead you back to the site of prior work. You may discover just how fleeting appreciation of your efforts and fidelity of the interventions can be: You may feel that you have been drawn into a time warp, coming out back at the beginning of your project—especially if staff turnover has cost you your allies.

Is there a solution? Probably not, for most educational reforms seem to change markedly over time no matter how precisely they are described. Designing your research to be longitudinal will assure that you maintain some control for a period of time, however. Such research allows you to track progress of children over a meaningful time period with regular follow-up. In some instances, simply having school personnel know that you will be back to collect follow-up data can change their behavior. (Note that it is a symbol of your commitment to your work, especially if you let them know that you will also provide refresher training for them. We have found that school staff are more willing to participate and to take you and your ideas seriously if you are in it for the long haul.)

Practically, if you anticipate having any interest in collecting long-term follow-up data, you might at least note during discussions with school staff that you would potentially like to obtain access at a later time, although long-term effectiveness is not your primary goal (if it were, your design would be longitudinal from the beginning). Be clear that you are not asking for a definite commitment, but potentially are interested in finding out what happens to your interventions after a period of time has passed.

RESEARCH IN THE CONTEXT OF SCHOOL CHANGE

Despite frequent complaints that schools are so bureaucratized that they cannot respond to the demands of today's society and children and are incapable of improving themselves without a radical transformation (see Schanker, 1990), researchers hoping to find a stable environment in which to conduct their research may find the number and rapidity of changes within schools mind-boggling. Many of the changes will be seen as mundane by school personnel, such as changing basal reader series or curricula or even the daily schedule; thus, they may react, "Heck, we do it all the time." Such changes may nonetheless be of major importance to researchers. Other changes may be viewed by all parties as major structural changes and heavily impact school personnel as well as researchers. These include school consolidations or expansions, school redistricting, attendance zone redistricting, school desegregation, the development of magnet schools, shifts to site-based management or outcome-based education, commitment to multicultural educational approaches, or implementing open enrollment policies. Regardless of whether changes are viewed as just tinkering with the system or as major structural alterations, to the extent that they change the environment and the activities within it, they affect the research efforts that go on within the schools.

We begin our discussion with small changes, ones that school staff may fail even to notice, but that can markedly change the baseline for research. For example, imagine that you are working on an intervention to improve reading of low-achieving children, with control classes that use traditional basal reader approaches to reading. Assume further that your approach relies heavily upon children learning to read using materials that are fun and meaningful to them. Then imagine that during your intervention the school district moves to a new reading series that stresses the same principles that you have stressed and that attempts to make reading fun and meaningful.

School research can be disrupted by many subtle influences that educators may not consider important enough to think about or to inform you about. Insofar as the goal of schools is to educate their children in the ways staff members believe are best for the children, constant change should be the rule rather than the exception. In fact, many critics would like to see changes occurring even more rapidly than they do now. As a researcher, you need to do what you can to bring up any questions that will help you to find out about the supposedly irrelevant changes that affect you. In the above example, your could find out in advance the schedule for changing basal reader series or approaches by talking to the district and building curriculum people. Once again, as a general strategy imagining yourself as a detective trying to uncover hidden clues may be helpful.

Major school transformations are great opportunities to study school change and innovation. But if you are already studying something else, reassignment of students to different schools or programs can destroy your sample and the integrity of your treatment. Fortunately, most structural changes like desegregation, school pairings, open enrollment programs, and the like occur in the fall, so studies conducted within school years are less likely to be affected by them. Shifts to outcome-based education or to site-based management can easily occur within school years, however; in fact, the changes may slowly evolve across entire school years. Further, such changes may not be visible to external observers unless those changes receive public attention. Changes in curricula, such as implementation of multicultural approaches to education, may also be less visible.

In sum, it is probably worthwhile to assume that schools are continually changing, even if the ones in which you are working prove to be exceptions. Only with such a perspective will you be able to plan for and anticipate the unexpected. Changes, however bothersome, remind us that the primary goal of schools is educating effectively, and that regardless of how much that goal is facilitated by research, there will be instances in which that goal is not compatible with the research we want to do.

8

Implementing the Research: Hoping for the Best and Coping With the Worst

In this chapter we address implementation. We attempt to describe not only issues to consider but also some responses to those issues, drawing on experiences of many of our colleagues as well as our own experience. An additional illustrative account of issues encountered in implementing an intervention project is provided by Solomon, Watson, Schapps, Battistich, and Solomon (1990).

We begin this chapter by discussing basic issues of implementation, then focus on responding to problems that emerge, and end with a look at the "problems" as opportunities to capitalize on the serendipity that may appear when unique circumstances present themselves.

BASIC ISSUES OF IMPLEMENTATION

To help you set up research so it is impeded as little as possible by problems that can emerge, we address (a) things to look for when attempting to assess your success in implementing your intervention, (b) issues of study evolution versus maintaining treatments without modification, (c) the importance of maintaining staff commitment to the project, (d) the value of assessing subtle and indirect effects of your treatments, (e) contrasts between researcher and educator views of program implementation, and, finally, (f) how research is necessarily embedded within the broader context of what is happening in schools.

Judging Successful Implementation of the Intervention. What can we do to help assure that our intervention gets as fair a test as is possible? There are at least two components involved. First, we need to be able to judge the *intent of the participants,* and second, we need to judge their *capability* to carry out their part of the research successfully.

96

Judging intent is potentially complex, but can be illustrated through a series of questions that you might ask. Initially, do the people who are supposed to be implementing the intervention know as much as they need to about how to do what they have to do and are they in fact attempting to do it? (Recall at thi
s point the earlier chapter on teacher types as you attempt to judge understanding and willingness.) Can you count on the staff? In particular, will staff members who are expected to participate in the study in fact put in the time needed to prepare for the intervention and then devote the needed and expected class time for conducting the study? Or will they forget to prepare and then attempt to "wing it," with consequent loss of precision? Worse yet, will they "forget" to conduct certain parts of the intervention or omit collection of a subset of the needed measures? Will they keep to the time schedule you have set, or might they be unconcerned about that and other "small" issues? (We will address some of these points in the third section of this chapter.)

At this stage it would not be surprising for you to find yourself frustrated at the minimal amount of time that school staff members put into projects, even if they have been involved from the start and have repeatedly expressed interest in and concern about your research. Remember that they have many competing demands on their time and that some of them really do not understand research. Nonetheless, you need their cooperation and will likely fail in your efforts without it. As a consequence, maintaining the external motivators (your presence, peer influences through colleagues modeling and talking about the project) is necessary for keeping up their willingness to participate.

You also need to be able to judge fairly quickly participants' competence to carry out the intent of your study. Where the first point focused on the "are" question, namely, are they trying to do it, this one focuses on the "can" question—can they successfully accomplish their roles (for an illustration of both issues, see Solomon et al., 1990).

Consider an illustration of each of the two questions, beginning with the "are" question: Have you screened out the crusty veterans or, if they are participating, have they been co-opted or at least neutralized? If the answer is no, they may well undermine your study either deliberately or through lack of interest (i.e., sins both of commission and omission) as they would anything else that they find worthless. As an illustration of the "can" question: Have the concrete thinkers been given enough specifics to enable them to proceed on their own without constantly calling you for help and advice? If not, their apprehension or perceived inability to have the answers to questions may lead them just to ignore your study or to change it so it makes sense to them.

One final important point related to teacher competence is the role that you envision for teachers. A researcher who expects teachers to understand the principles underlying and embedded within the treatment needs to develop a much higher level of understanding on the part of participants than one who expects teachers to function solely as technicians implementing an intervention "by the numbers." There are benefits to be gained from the first type of training. Whereas the latter type of researcher expects teachers only to follow the script and seek advice when things need to be altered, the former type of researcher should be better prepared to cope with the range of unpredictable events that can (and often do) occur on a daily basis with teachers able to respond on their own while still maintaining the integrity of the treatment.

To summarize, both capability and willingness are important issues to examine, for a researcher needs both cooperative and skilled individuals to help carry out the study. In some instances, teacher enthusiasm is diminished by lack of understanding, in others understanding is worthless since it is accompanied by resistance to the approaches that are being used. Unfortunately, some researchers too readily assume that (a) once training has occurred and plans are in place things are going well, and (b) if no questions are being raised, then the issues are well understood. From our perspective, such assumptions need frequently to be checked.

Study Evolution Versus Maintaining "Intact" Programs. A major dilemma for educational researchers is balancing the educational goal of enhancing the learning of all students against the scientific goal of letting the treatment run its course without varying it in any substantive way. In some instances, the welfare of students may suggest an early termination of your study because positive effects are not visible, in others an early termination may seem desirable because the intervention is working so successfully that you want to give it to the control group as well. If the treatment turns out to be a powerful one, its expanded implementation may not wait for you or anyone else to declare the study a success. Teachers are likely to talk about the intervention in places like the teachers' lounge. In schools that contain both treatment and control classrooms, and in particular, where individual teachers teach both targeted and control children, there is great danger of diffusion of the intervention. In other words, if the treatment works well, teachers may try to use it or variations of it in their other classes or control teachers may pick up aspects of the treatments. Unfortunately, the control and treatment conditions then become more similar than they should be, which potentially diminishes the likelihood of your finding significant positive effects from the treatment (for an example, see Aronson & Osherow, 1980).

The potential problem is much more than simply what teachers want to do. Experienced researchers respond to pressures to enhance the learning of all children in widely varying ways. For example, as researchers get involved with the classrooms in which they are working, they often develop relationships with the teachers and children that make it difficult for them personally to continue treatments that don't seem to be working. Even though there are strong scientific reasons for researchers to want to maintain a study as it is planned, there are also strong practical reasons for being responsive to external pressures.

Even if things are not going well, however, how do you—or anyone else—decide whether the unfavorable effects that you are witnessing are due to your treatment? Maybe the treatment is not responsible for the effects or has only accelerated the rate at which students reach a point of personal frustration; even without your study they might inevitably have to experience and then deal with the frustration. In other words, things that worry you because you feel responsible for them may be unrelated to and unaffected by your research.

So you might decide that you should ignore the anecdotal evidence and maintain fidelity of the intervention rather than prejudging it. After all, even effective treatments don't all show dramatic effects, particularly at the beginning. Isn't some disruption to be expected when one starts something new or changes their approach?

But how much disruption of student learning is acceptable? At what point should one put the educational needs of the children before the scientific needs of the researcher? Here we get to the crux of the issue, namely, that as much as you hope that you never have to confront a situation like the one described, you need to be prepared to make choices between your scientific needs and the educational needs of children.

At the same time, however, it is important to remember that conflict between research and learning is not inevitable; you knew there were good reasons to work with school staff in planning for your research. We have stressed planning for the research in conjunction with school staff for a number of reasons, and perhaps have not given this one its due: Simply, teachers bring with them a very practical orientation to school issues. Given their experience, they should have pretty good ideas about how students will react to most types of interventions. Listening to their ideas and suggestions before the study begins should lessen considerably your chances of experiencing such problems.

The issue of how to respond to student outcomes can, however, go much deeper and involve your underlying philosophy about how to do educational research. At one extreme are the researchers who place control of and responsibility for interventions in the hands of school staff. In its worst form, this means sacrificing control of the conceptual variables that are involved and engaging in atheoretical program evaluation research. In a more rigorous form, it means recognizing that teachers and school personnel will do what they want once you are gone and probably even while you are still there, so you might as well try to work incrementally, providing them with broad principles and then letting them determine, with your assistance and guidance, how those principles are best implemented.

At the other extreme are researchers who demand total control over the environments in which they work. In its worst form, such research brings intact into any classroom "the model." "The model" is an intervention that has worked before and is assumed to be immediately translatable to any other classroom. It's the old "Take it or leave it. If you want it, you want it my way." In a more typical form, this type of research comes from researchers who are concerned about theory development and willing to demand from school staff that, once agreed upon, the study will go as planned barring major disasters.

As we hope has become apparent, we do not believe that there is a single correct or even "best" solution to this problem. We are partial to the "action research" tradition (see Lewin, 1946) that uses the most current theoretical developments to impact on practice and applied-setting research to inform and improve theory. That tradition tends to move us toward the position of maintaining fidelity of treatment so the theoretical importance of the study can be assessed. Nonetheless, we recognize that there are times when it may be necessary to change plans to react to events that are occurring, and that such changes are not necessarily bad.

Consider as an example the experiences of a colleague of ours who currently is conducting a study designed to improve the reading skills of first-grade children who are at risk of failing to learn to read by the end of first grade. The study has treatment classes at one school and control classes at another, which diminishes the likelihood of diffusion of treatment. (Interestingly, however, there seems to be another type of diffusion of treatment in that study, for the children identified as "average" readers, who are not getting special reading instruction, seem to be attending closely to the special instruction of the low-achieving children and consequently are achieving at a level far exceeding their peers at the control school despite having no formal intervention and being similar on the pretest.) By the end of February, about 70% of the low-achieving children at the target school were successfully reading, compared with 10% of the comparable group at the control school.

From the perspective of what is best for the students: Should our colleague halt the study and attempt to train teachers at the other school to use the techniques, or wait until next school year with its new sample of first graders? Are current practices acceptable for one more year, with the control school simply continuing to instruct children in the same ways it has over the recent past? From the perspective of what is best for the research: Would finding out how effectively the techniques work in a short time period be as important as finding out how they work over an entire school year? (Note that we here revisit the issue of duration of studies.) Would colleagues criticize the study findings if the treatment were successfully applied to the control school and then the positive effects of treatment were lost? (In other words, would they accept a baseline from noncomparable schools as documenting success of the treatment? The answer, of course, is that some would not.) Clearly, the issues are complex and probably not resolvable by consensual decision making. Being aware of them, however, can help you plan for the unexpected and develop contingencies that keep the study meaningful even if it faces changes.

Maintaining Staff Commitment. We have already spent a considerable amount of time encouraging researchers to attempt to develop exchange types of relationships with school staff, and there is really little to add here. Researchers who study interaction patterns of groups might note the importance of revisiting process issues, that is, checking to be sure that the individuals involved feel that what was agreed to is being carried out. Most important for the researcher is that once you have commitment and cooperation you do as much as you can to maintain it. Part of maintaining commitment comes from appearing to be open to issues raised by staff and from responding flexibly to concerns. For example, be willing to compromise on nonessential features of the design; such behavior will help to maintain rapport without threatening treatment integrity. Appearing to be rigid is one way to lose the commitment that you worked hard to obtain.

Even though specific approaches involved in maintaining commitment of teachers and other school staff may change from study to study, there are some general guidelines you might consider:

- Build teams or support groups to work on your project so individuals receive help and encouragement as well as social pressure to continue.
- Be available for questions at the beginning of the study so things begin fairly smoothly; remain available in case problems arise.
- Make sure that your allies know what they can do to help maintain staff enthusiasm.
- Set up mechanisms so staff have avenues to provide feedback and suggestions.

To illustrate how and why the specific approaches to maintaining enthusiasm can vary so greatly, consider a contrast between schools in which there is only a single ongoing research project and ones that experience a continuing flow of researchers and research ideas. There are definite advantages in being the only show in town—staff commitment should be much easier to maintain than if staff energy and interest are regularly redirected toward new ideas.

As a second illustration, consider the contrast between work at a single site and work that has multiple replications in different buildings. Single-site research allows the researchers to spend more time keeping track of and paying attention to the staff and their concerns, which can imbue a sense of specialness along with the greater intensiveness and scrutiny. In other words, single sites provide a greater sense of control and support for and concern about staff, which can be used to keep up staff motivation and commitment. Multiple sites offer other benefits: Staff members do not feel that they live and work under a microscope. They are freer to behave "normally." Note that "normal" behavior may generalize better to other schools and circumstances. In addition, there may be less danger of contamination of treatment, particularly if some of the treatments are done across sites. Finally, multiple sites can provide opportunities to develop cross-building networks and support groups as well as interbuilding competitions to see which building can best implement the intervention. In sum, the dynamics change considerably when multiple sites are used. Specific techniques for maintaining motivation will likely vary depending upon the number of sites selected. For example, the specialness that exists in single-site studies can be matched in multiple-site studies through interbuilding cooperation and competition and through reinforcing staff members' perceptions that they are being treated as valued participants in the research process.

Assessing Subtle Effects of Interventions. Even though we all hope for strong effects like those reported by our colleague's reading intervention program, most educational interventions produce much more modest effects. In fact, the effects of some interventions may be invisible on the measures that were supposed to document them. In this section we focus on things you can do to increase the likelihood of assessing successfully any effects that appear.

A good starting point is provided by Campbell (1969) in his article "Reforms as Experiments." He notes that positive effects of almost any reform can be gathered as long as one is willing to seek out testimonials and other anecdotal evidence. Our position is slightly different, for as much as we may need testimonials to provide upbeat conclusions to report back to school staff, as researchers we do not want to promote strategies and methods that don't work. At the same time, we don't want to miss important positive effects that occur, particularly if we miss them because our instruments are imprecise or are focused on the wrong places.

Consider, for example, our study of the effects of different approaches on the learning of low-achieving students. Even in such a study where the focus is on student learning, it is worthwhile to include data focused on the teachers involved and on the climate of the building. Some of our more interesting findings appeared on the variables that described building and classroom climate. Examples of the types of measures that might be worth collecting (these depend somewhat on the focus of the particular study) are observational data on classrooms and staff behavior patterns; teacher attitude measures; and measures of teacher interactions and school culture. Of particular importance are measures of how staff members think about, feel about, and judge the intervention; as people say about political arenas, "Perception is reality." In other words, what school staff perceive can be real insofar as their perceptions shape what they remember, regardless of the empirical findings that you or other researchers report.

Finally, even "unsuccessful" studies can produce substantial and meaningful effects. For example, an intervention without documentable positive effects on students may still be a success if it expands the range of curricular approaches that the teachers involved will consider using. That is, if it plants the seeds for changing teacher behavior patterns in ways that benefit the students, it may be a major success. Some teachers have very entrenched ways of thinking about what they do; in certain instances, those ways have endured over years despite the emergence of many new ideas and approaches. Just getting such teachers to consider changing their ways may be a major accomplishment.

To sum up, it is important to consider potential diffuse and subtle effects. To the extent that additional data are collected, they can augment the primary and more direct findings in important ways.

Researcher Versus Educator Interests. We believe that in most instances the goals of school personnel who are interested in research are compatible with the goals of researchers. Nevertheless, we have encountered instances in which researcher beliefs about what makes good educational policy can have adverse political and economic effects on schools. Thus, even if school personnel are in general eager to change their behavior patterns to follow educational innovation, they may face conflicts that make them less receptive to particular aspects of the research process. Importantly, their behaviors are in part determined by government, state, and school district policies that dictate ways of behaving and organizing information; those policies, for example, affect the monies that schools and districts receive.

Researchers working with special populations are particularly likely to encounter such conflicts. For example, many researchers view the process of labeling students (e.g., learning disabled, mildly mentally handicapped, or behavior disordered) as not useful in designing compensatory programs. Conducting research on the labeling process is not, however, without risks. For example, schools that participate in research that (a) treats the children so the labels no longer apply, (b) shows that the labels do not lead to educational programs that work consistently for any group of children, or (c) invalidates the entire labeling process risk losing the support of federal or state policymakers who have decided that particular monies should be set aside to give only to children who have been identified as fitting under specific category labels. If the number of children in a school or district classified into those disability categories decreases, then the district may be no longer eligible for the money dedicated to the problems faced by those children and their teachers. Thus, efforts that redefine children out of categories or that point to shortcomings in the way those categories are defined may be costly to the district or school and may result in less money being available to help children with problems. Put bluntly, good and sensitive research may result in poorer educational practices insofar as policies are insensitive to efforts to provide the best possible education for all children. In such instances, it may be acceptable to conduct labeling research, but the policy implications of that research are likely to be ignored insofar as implementation has financial costs.

Similarly, teachers may face situations in which behaviors that provide positive social messages to children simultaneously deny those children access to services and support staff that would be useful both to the children and to the teachers. Removing stigmatizing labels probably has beneficial social effects on children; at the same time, because those children no longer are labeled, they no longer qualify for special services that accompany the labels. Thus, a decision may mean choosing between positive social effects and fiscal support.

Viewing Research From a Broader Context. As we focus on the details of our work, it is easy to forget that our work is being conducted within a dynamic environment that experiences and mirrors the issues, problems, and difficulties of society. Thus, as we search for small victories, we need to remember that large battles are continually being fought. However humbling such thinking may be, it is important insofar as the broad social conditions facing schools severely limit the range and scope of any accomplishments. Children who are malnourished, who are experiencing adverse effects of poverty, who are addicted to drugs or affected by impacts of drug use by family members, whose parents fight daily or abuse them, or who are homeless may not be affected either by your intervention or by any intervention that doesn't address their underlying problems.

As we go into schools, there is a sense of privilege that we are granted, namely, that we may be allowed to address some relatively esoteric or nominal problem without being asked to help address the major problems and difficulties that recur daily. From such a perspective, it is not surprising to find that our work has relatively low priority and seems to be given much less energy than we might hope. Nonetheless, to the extent that we extend our work or engage our colleagues to address the major problems present in schools, our privilege may be one that produces effects beyond those expected. For example, if we attempt to observe and examine the range of prominent influences present in schools, we should begin to identify the complex array of variables that influence our research. Thus, follow-up efforts will in many instances extend our work in ways that broaden its impact (e.g., that make it more socially relevant) and that deal directly with the factors that limit it. It is to be hoped that many of us will bring our insights to bear on the problems of schools regardless of whether those problems were the ones that we initially identified for our research; even if our work does not broaden beyond our initial focus, our later attempts should benefit from our better understanding of the dynamics of schools.

WHAT HAPPENS WHEN THINGS GO WRONG

Although careful planning can smooth considerably the difficulties that we encounter when implementing our interventions, there inevitably will be problems. They can be created by us: Our instructions may be unclear, our instruments may accidentally omit a page of questions or change the wording of specific set of items across administration times, some of the questionnaires may be put together incorrectly, too few copies of the instruments may be sent to particular schools, or a sample may be found insufficient or unbalanced (e.g., failing to allow for reasonable attrition rates for longitudinal research or to sample enough students of particular types).

Problems for researchers also can be created by circumstances of schools: Innovation within schools can markedly change the nature of the student experiences, funding problems can change plans and programs within schools, teacher or principal transfers and promotions can dramatically alter the major players in the school, teacher unionization can lead to reconfiguration of teacher responsibilities, or administrative reorganizations can reconfigure the available sites.

A third source of problems is individuals' circumstances: Parents move, taking their children out of the school, teachers take leaves of absence or even quit their positions, or problems like long-term illnesses nonrandomly remove children from our sample.

Finally, there are chance occurrences that are rare yet potentially devastating. These types of events include fires that force the closing of entire school buildings (as actually happened in a school desegregation study with which one of us was involved), snow storms or power blackouts preventing travel and closing particular schools on the day that the data are to be collected, or viruses like the flu decimating the sample at our most critical time.

Remember Murphy's Law: Everything that can go wrong. . . . Even if you are thinking that you knew things were going too smoothly and that there were going to be some more catches, well, remember, problems can also be opportunities. Before we try to recast problems as opportunities, however, we will cover the more basic issue of coping and moving ahead.

Once again, we use as an illustration our study of low-achieving elementary school children. As described earlier, we were attempting to compare three different programs that worked with children in regular classes with programs that worked primarily with low-achieving children in special programs outside the regular classroom. In the case of one intervention, we were forced at the last minute to change the entire set of schools because we lost the school district that was to provide the schools for that intervention. Of the replacement schools, two had not begun to implement the intervention at the time when our study began. They were a problem insofar as all other schools had been working with their programs for at least a couple of years, so the people at those other schools had the time to learn better what they were doing and to sort out the problems. In other words, if we had found a weaker (or in any major way different) effect of the treatment in our replacement schools, we would never know the extent to which our findings reflected the lesser experience of school staff with the program. This potential problem forced us to approach the situation differently, analyzing the data in ways that allowed us to examine the effects of the different circumstances.

A second issue that arose was that in order to find additional schools that were using one of our interventions, we had to take urban schools, although all 10 other schools were suburban, in small towns, or rural. Given the marked differences of racial and ethnic composition, social class, district bureaucracy, and student backgrounds, direct comparisons were greatly complicated.

The broad point here is that researchers need to think about contingencies and plan to take an approach that deals successfully with problems that arise. Insofar as the problems are frequently unpredictable both as to types that occur and their severity, it is virtually impossible to plan specifically for them. Rather, we argue for the importance of taking an approach that transmits to participants the message that encountering problems is part of life and that problems like the ones we described typically can be handled successfully. The image requires being flexible, adaptable, and upbeat; the approach needs to be a constructive one.

In other words, having to change your plans will likely complicate your life and your data analyses, but major inconveniences are no reason to panic and look about for targets for blame and wrath. Rather, problems require you to be more thoughtful and to consider alternative explanations for your findings. Our approach focuses on carefully considering consequences and developing alternative ways to get to the questions that need to be addressed and that try to dismiss alternative explanations. Once again detective imagery seems appropriate.

This section began by focusing on the sources of problems because we wanted to remind readers that many problems originate during the planning of the research. Careful planning and active participation by school staff will help to minimize problems along the way. School staff should be particularly helpful in anticipating conflicts.

Finally, no section on problems would be complete without a warning about tight time lines and tight controls. Tight time lines are an invitation to problems, particularly in a location where weather problems can lead to school closings and disrupt researcher travel plans. Even without weather problems, however, schools move on a schedule that makes little sense to most outsiders. When holidays, vacations, compensatory time off, meetings, and parent conferences are factored in, it may seem that children are out of school as much as they are in school. Researchers who expect predictable and consistent schedules like those found at universities will likely be dismayed.

One other way to think about schools is to view them as being much like the children within them: They move at the rate they feel like moving and sometimes don't complete everything they plan to complete. This statement is not intended to imply that educators are childlike or irresponsible; rather, schools that are particularly sensitive to the needs of their students may create problems for researchers as the staff attempt to keep learning meaningful, particularly if keeping it meaningful means being flexible and, if necessary, rearranging lesson plans and schedules. For example, changing the curriculum in response to the war with Iraq or changes in Eastern Europe might disrupt school researchers, yet not responding to major world events transmits the wrong message about the importance, relevance, and usefulness of education.

OPPORTUNISM IN EDUCATIONAL RESEARCH

The war with Iraq provides an excellent opportunity for us to switch the focus to irreplaceable opportunities that may come along during our research. The Gulf War gave teachers of geography and history unparalleled opportunities to demonstrate in meaningful ways how important it is for children to learn these subjects. If we were fortunate enough to be doing research on a topic like children's understanding of places in the world, we would have had a ready-made longitudinal study of the impacts of war on student interest and learning. We might also have had unusual opportunities even if we were working far afield from those topics; for example, research focusing on personal adjustment or anxieties in children would have great potential to assess and document changes in student attitudes and concerns.

Education frequently uses terms or phrases to highlight and transmit ideas; a term to capture the essence of what we have been describing is *researchable moments*. It transmits the notion that if we can get past the stage of whining about our problems, we might realize that "one person's headache is another's joy," namely, that something even more interesting may come from our being advantageously situated and mobilized to collect data. To benefit from opportunities, however, one needs to be able to look broadly at what is happening and what the respective costs and benefits are of changes that might occur.

In our study of low-achieving children, our site problem resulted in our sample including two inner-city schools, which in numerous ways enriched our sample and drew our attention to some problems that we otherwise would not have addressed. For example, the way definitions were used in some of the other sites to classify students would have resulted in virtually all of the students from one school being classified as needing special education services. Attention to issues of classification was forced on us by the presence of sites in which the use of categories was clearly and markedly different from other sites.

At a very different level, any study that collects substantial information from schools may provide useful and important baseline information for future research. Our study of low-achieving students provided us with baseline data on students and staff from more than 30 schools that were participating in school effectiveness research. Thus, in the event that we were to become aware of any future efforts of those schools to dramatically alter their programs, it would be relatively easy for us to revisit those schools. In fact, some of them are currently initiating programs in areas like outcome-based education that may lead us back to them in future research, yet for reasons far removed from the ones that led us there in the first place.

Overall, then, our discussion has attempted to suggest that sometimes seemingly little things that just happen to occur at fortuitous times may provide unparalleled opportunities and should not be wasted. Most of us are likely to experience at best only limited opportunities, but it makes sense to keep a broad perspective and to be prepared to mobilize efforts quickly to respond to opportunities. We often realize far too late how great the opportunities were that we missed. To return to the Gulf War, it will be interesting to see in publications during the early 1990s how many of our colleagues took advantage of the war with Iraq to investigate meaningful educational and social issues.

EXERCISES

11. *Judging Teacher Intent and Competence*. Review your prior exercises and select an implementation study for this exercise. Refer back to suggested questions about teacher intent and competence. Which ones would you use for your example? Are additional questions needed?

12. *Personal Beliefs About Study Changes*. Review the section "Study Evolution Versus Maintaining 'Intact' Programs." What would you prefer to do if you were conducting the reading intervention study? What is your personal view about the importance of maintaining fidelity of treatment? If possible, divide into groups of four, with two persons favoring changing and two favoring maintaining the treatment. Have all four advocate first for maintaining the treatment. Then switch and all four advocate changing it.

9

Data Analysis and Interpretation: What Does It All Mean?

Finally, the end of the line—almost. All the instruments have been administered and returned, we have coped satisfactorily with some unexpected problems, and we have even cleaned up any messes that we made. Now we just need to take care of data coding, data entry, data analyses, and data interpretation and we will be finished. Most important, we're back on familiar ground, working in our offices and at home via the magic of microcomputers and modems. Although the specific analyses that we perform will reflect our theoretical perspectives, our practical concerns, and the dynamics of school settings, issues of data coding, data entry, and data analysis differ little from those issues with nonschool data sets and therefore we will not cover them here.

Instead we will focus on data interpretation, in which the issues may differ considerably from those that stem from basic research or from other applied research. We discuss ways of presenting results, interpreting results, and communicating findings to both the academic community and to policymakers and other practitioners. Finally, we look back to see how much time it has taken us to conclude our research.

PRESENTING RESULTS

For research conducted in educational settings, results need to be viewed from and interpreted within three frames of reference. First, as with any theoretical work, there is the *conceptual importance* of the work to consider. At a specific level, one needs to present the findings in such a way that their fit with prior research can be assessed; more generally, the findings need to be presented in ways that make clear whether they advance the theory as you had hoped or anticipated that they would. (Stating and directly addressing specific conceptually derived hypotheses is helpful.) For example, the research questions addressed might examine whether patterns of findings suggest limiting conditions

111

for, or limited applicability of, prior research. Alternatively, they might provide information on how the theory can be extended in new and important directions. Such questions could include: Does the work provide a conceptual replication or extension of past work? Do we know anything new about the theory as a result of your study?

Unfortunately, real-world research too often encounters practical obstacles that can obscure effects of interventions, allowing only complex and yet tentative conclusions with respect to underlying theories. Educational researchers should not expect findings like those of our colleague whose study lifted the rate of reading competence from 10% of the low-achieving students to more than 70% of them. More commonly, the pattern of empirical findings will yield little clarity. For example, our study of low-achieving children established no approach to be clearly superior to the others; rather, we found large variability across sites and classes within conditions. Even our more limited and specific types of analyses defied straightforward interpretation.

In circumstances where the findings are strong, they should be presented to speak clearly and strongly about the effectiveness of the conceptual framework that underlies the intervention. Judging from our experience, the results sections of the strong studies are the easiest ones to write. Excessive complexity in presenting the results may reflect difficulties in interpreting the patterns of the findings.

The second issue to address is the *practical importance* of the work. The issue here is how the data analyses address practical and applied questions, namely, whether the research will affect the ways things are done in schools or other educational settings. Your results might focus on the following questions: Are there strong implications of your research for the ways education is practiced? Based upon your findings, are there ways in which educational approaches can be modified to be made more effective? Are there particular recommendations to be drawn from your work that could help schools when they have to confront problems?

Third, an important consideration and one that has received a substantial amount of attention recently is the *magnitude of the effects* of the intervention (see Cooper, 1989). Because attaining significant differences depends heavily upon sample size and with large samples even modest differences may be significant, estimating the strength of the effect has become an integral part of the reporting of results. Reporting strength of effects is particularly important in an applied area like education, for information on the strength of effect helps policymakers to construct cost/benefit analyses. For example, the body of research on cooperative learning has found a typical subject in the cooperative condition to score at the 78th percentile of an individualistic comparison group (see, e.g., Johnson et al., 1981); such findings can be extrapolated to estimate the size of anticipated improvement on a particular task or subject area as well as the percentage of subjects in that condition who exceed the average of the comparison group. As a second example, educational demographers frequently contrast the cost of one year of education with one year of incarceration. Educational interventions dealing with youth who are at risk for criminal behavior can be presented as reducing criminal behavior, and the costs of the intervention compared with reduced costs of incarceration.

Presenting estimates of strength of effects is not new, for there are the traditional statistical estimates representing the amount of variance explained, like eta squared, omega squared, and R squared. More recently, however, researchers have developed and refined approaches that are intended to facilitate research synthesis; these approaches have been called meta-analysis (see Glass, 1976, 1977). Meta-analytic approaches have presented the differences between conditions as what have been called effect sizes (see, e.g., Cooper, 1989). Effect sizes present the differences in terms of how many standard deviations the condition means are apart from one another; for example, a difference with an effect size of .5 would mean that the groups differed by half a standard deviation. Cooper (1989) provides an excellent introduction to meta-analysis techniques (see also Rosenthal, 1984).

DRAWING INFERENCES ABOUT YOUR FINDINGS

Inferences can be drawn at a number of levels. First, they reflect your preferred construction of the meaning and implications of specific findings. In that context, they are hypothesis specific, that is, they present your interpretation of the meaning of results in terms of specific practical and conceptual hypotheses. They address questions like: Did your intervention work? How can teachers be made to work together more effectively? What type of principal gets the best productivity and the highest morale from his or her teachers? Does Theory A account for the data more effectively than does Theory B?

Second, inferences can speak broadly about meanings that you impute to your findings and the implications of those findings. As a hypothetical example, in our study of low-achieving children, we might have wanted to suggest that certain strategies are particularly effective, or that teaching low-achieving children in the mainstream is better than teaching them in separate pullout classrooms, or that schools concerned about the achievements of their low-achieving children ought to use the strategies and approaches that we did. We could even go so far as to speculate wildly about the value and importance of our work.

In other words, the inference stage (normally found in the discussion section of manuscripts) attempts to give meaning to one's findings and to tie them back to the broad issues that provided the rationale for that work in the first place. In such a study this would be the place to interpret the findings, sort out the various competing predictions, tie back to broader theoretical views and policy perspectives, discuss any additional policy implications of the work, and speculate about subsequent steps.

In educational research, there are two major groups of people for whom you may be drawing inferences. The first is inferences directed toward researchers like yourself. The second is inferences directed toward practitioners who might want to know what you think your research means. The two types of inferences are very different from one another. In the first case you are fairly free to recommend whatever you believe logically follows from your work, because you know that your skeptical peers will not take your ideas on faith (they are more likely to disagree with you and attempt to design an experiment that shows you are wrong). In the latter case, however, you need to remember that a large part of your audience may take what you say on faith; they lack the technical knowledge and skills to draw reasonable meaning from your work given the limitations of the research design and the findings.

For example, in the health field there are strong public pressures to follow any conspicuous empirical findings by immediate changes in medical practice. Unfortunately, most findings are followed fairly quickly by some contradictory findings, which then throw the public into confusion and uncertainty about what they should do. Note that a major issue here seemingly is that the nonscientific audience has a difficult if not impossible time in distinguishing (a) recommendations based upon widely accepted principles coupled with appreciable research support from (b) recommendations based upon a single potentially idiosyncratic study. Further, the difficulties are exacerbated when the recommendations are consistent with what the public would like to believe or seem to offer health opportunities that were not previously available.

In the field of education, the costs of overzealous inferences are about as great as those in health fields. Simply, your interpretations may be taken out of context and used politically to argue for certain approaches in ways that you would never consider supporting. Even if your inferences are not used irresponsibly, they still may be interpreted as providing a much stronger endorsement for a particular strategy than you had intended. If there is a good chance that practitioners will be reading your work, it is probably wise to embed the practical implications of your work carefully within the existing literature and prevailing techniques, and to interpret the findings in ways that temper the enthusiasm of naive readers.

COMMUNICATING YOUR FINDINGS

As academics are generally familiar with the traditional ways of communicating one's findings to the research community (e.g., conference presentations, working papers, monographs, and finally, refereed articles), our focus is on the less familiar, namely, communicating with schools and policymakers. We distinguish between those two groups because we believe an important part of the communication process is to give schools information that will help them but not punish them; information provided to policymakers should help them to make the best decisions regardless of what they are currently doing. In other words, policymakers need to look beyond their specific cases to how various approaches work generally; if they primarily focus on their own individual programs, they may lose the big picture and accept suboptimal decisions or retain programs that over the long term should be modified or changed.

Feedback to Schools

Our general strategy in providing feedback to schools is to keep it as straightforward and descriptive as possible, and provide it in as timely a fashion as is possible. For example, in our study of low-achieving students we provided information about staff climate measures to each school in a way that each one had only the data from its own school plus the mean and standard deviation of the entire sample. In that way we hoped to focus attention on how the school stood compared to all other schools, but avoid comparisons with other individual buildings. We presented profiles across the 15 school effectiveness characteristics rather than attempting to summarize the data any further in order to keep the comparisons multidimensional and, we hoped, to allow each school to define and focus on its own strengths and shortcomings. We also provided only aggregate information rather than any information about individuals. (For an example, see Figure 9.1.) Note that the dashed line is the grand mean across all 15 characteristics and the large dots the means across schools for each characteristic. For the feedback to each school, the school scores were marked by dots and connected across the characteristics.

Similarly, for the student achievement measures we provided grade-by-grade feedback to each school that allowed them to compare the performance of their students against the average of all other project schools. We scaled scores within each grade using the overall mean and standard deviation from our initial sample of more than 4,000 students randomly selected from each participating classroom. We set the mean for each grade to 100 and the standard deviation to 15, thus presenting scores in a relatively familiar metric. For the spring scores, we used the fall norms so that the feedback for each school could reflect the growth of its students. That is, a comparison of fall with spring scores yielded change from fall to spring on a common metric or scale because within each grade fall and spring scores were scaled using the same mean and standard deviation. (If we had scaled the spring performance scores the way we scaled fall scores, namely, establishing norms from that testing and using those norms to scale each school's scores, the overall mean across all schools would again have to be 100, which would make it appear to schools that overall there was no change or "improvement.")

Underlying our way of providing feedback was our desire not to present the data in a way that would encourage district administrators to use the data to punish schools or withhold money from them. Second, we wanted to minimize the kinds of insidious social comparisons that would allow school personnel to comment about how much better they were doing than people at some other school. Finally, by providing the feedback as quickly as we could (admittedly not always very fast), we hoped to give to schools the message that we felt that an important aspect

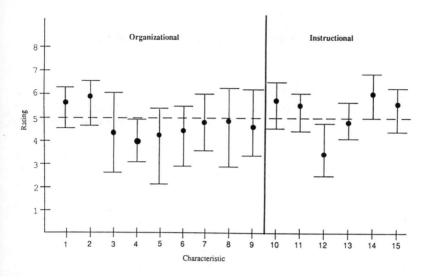

Figure 9.1. School Characteristics Survey (ScharS) Round 2 Results

KEY: – – Overall mean for 32 schools
      • Mean for 32 schools
    ⊥ Range of scores for 32 schools

NOTE: Means and range of scores for teacher ratings of 15 school effectiveness characteristics across 32 Minnesota Schools. Each school received its profile of scores on this page.

of our partnership was to give them information that they potentially could use for staff development or for curriculum assessment.

Feedback to Policymakers

If our major goal had been to influence the decisions of policymakers, our approach would have been very different from that described above. We would have focused on broad patterns of findings, particularly as they contrasted particular strategies or approaches. Our overall objective would have been to make as clear as possible the implications of using different approaches and the conditions under which each seemed to work best.

For example, earlier discussions of cooperative learning techniques noted their effectiveness (see Johnson et al., 1981). Nonetheless, for a period of time cooperative learning researchers argued over which of several approaches was "best," which had the effects both of taking attention away from the general effectiveness of those techniques and of confusing policymakers about which cooperative learning technique if any they would want to use. To the extent that studies from that literature were intended to be directed toward policymakers rather than the research community, the discussions should have focused on the overall effectiveness of the approaches rather than on their relative strengths and weaknesses.

As a second illustration, we revisit our study of low-achieving children. As we noted earlier, the findings contrasting various approaches to integrated education for special education students were generally equivocal; the major sources of variability were those that occurred across schools and classrooms regardless of the approach used. We were not surprised, because the schools were responsible for the implementation of the approaches; their effectiveness in implementing the conceptual approaches varied widely, and despite our efforts to create consistency across sites, they each implemented their own variations of the treatments. Thus, our study was not rich in implications regarding the best approach to use for integrating special education children, for it did not provide a particularly sensitive test of the theoretical principles underlying the various approaches. Nevertheless we were able to glean policy implications at two levels, the first regarding the broader issues of integrated versus pullout programs, the second from our smaller-scale comparisons across buildings with the same programs.

In concluding, we cannot overstate either the ethical importance of providing feedback in a constructive way to schools and administrators or the practical value to you if you plan to conduct further research in school settings. Clearly, feedback means more than sending a copy of the grant final report or published work to schools; it requires thinking creatively about the types of information that might be useful to schools and the best ways of presenting that information so it is intelligible to school staff and does not punish them for participating in research. Once again, discussions with school staff in planning the project might help to guide you in the types of information that staff members would find most useful. For policymakers, it is the pattern of findings that we believe is most important and useful; discussions that obscure the overall results by focusing on specific nuances of the research typically will not benefit policymakers.

HOW LONG DID IT TAKE TO GET DONE?

Before wrapping up, we look back one last time at the various steps and time we committed to the process. For this discussion, we assume that our plan is an intervention study of some moderate duration (e.g., 6-13 weeks); a one-shot, single-class, or limited-duration study might be accomplished much more simply. In what we view as a fairly comprehensive scenario of the steps involved, a study done in the schools

- begins with the definition of a problem that may have both theoretical and practical roots, moves then
- to a limited literature search
- to study planning and instrument development
- to gaining access to schools and meeting with school staff
- to making necessary modifications in instruments in order to fit the demands of class schedules and time
- to gaining approval from human subjects review panels
- to implementing the intervention and collecting the information
- to coding and analyzing the data, and finally
- ends with preparing the necessary reports so that professional colleagues and practitioners gain the feedback and information that they deserve

The literature search will of course vary depending upon the expertise of the researchers. Even with the advantages provided by modern data bases, novices should be prepared to spend at least one month to identify, locate, and read the relevant studies. Once you are familiar with the research literature, it is time to plan the study and tentatively develop the measures. We believe that another 2 to 4 weeks is a reasonable time line for individuals reasonably competent in research methodologies. Selection of certain measures that are difficult to obtain, however, can appreciably lengthen this stage.

As noted earlier, the school access time line is an interesting one because there are certain times during the school year that are most amenable to planning. Our experience has been that spring is the best time to plan research that is to be conducted during the next year, and that planning is essential if one expects to conduct intervention research that lasts for a substantial period of time. With spring planning, the study can begin as early as the following fall quarter (another general recommendation is to avoid the first few weeks of the school year because the teachers and students are still getting to know one another). During the spring, the study can be presented to and discussed with school staff, preliminary plans for any staff development activities can be developed, and the array of measures can be refined to fit within allocated class time. Get staff commitment at this stage. If we accept the time constraints recommended, working backward would suggest a starting date of January or February for the literature review.

During the summer, instruments can be finalized, materials prepared, any training procedures can be developed and rehearsed, and human subjects approval forms can be obtained. We recommend waiting until this stage to obtain human subject review because letters of support from school personnel will likely be required, and those would not be available until details are worked out with the participating schools.

Fall will be busy, beginning with staff development activities in September, then focusing on consent forms and premeasures that need to be administered. Finally, most research will need to be ready to start by the end of the calendar year, so final preparation is essential. Remember that due to school start-up time in the fall and the holiday season between Thanksgiving and Christmas, we earlier recommended the January to March period as being best for any 6 to 13 week intervention study.

Winter will likely be the season of the intervention, which commits you for as long as your study endures. After the conclusion of your study, you still have to allocate time for data coding, entry, and analysis; finally, time is needed for interpretation and write-up. In sum, from beginning to end a moderately complex intervention study is likely to take at least 1 and probably the better part of 2 years.

Well, now we are finally at the end. As you look back and think about what we have covered, you may have decided that we have been coopted, and have turned from typical social scientists with the usual types of theoretical concerns into education groupies interested in conducting research on educational problems. We're not sure whether or not we really are that, but it does seem to us that we have struggled with insider/outsider perspectives about doing research in educational settings versus doing educational research (the latter defined by its concern with the issues and problems that face education). We decided to mention this issue in closing only because we expect that it may have been a conflict experienced by many of the readers of this book as we focused on issues relevant to both types of research.

Given the way we have constructed the book, we feel that it would not be fitting to end with an altogether serious discussion. Rather, after all that we have vicariously endured, we would like, also vicariously, to toast the completion of this book and the progress of your research. We tried to cover a broad array of possible issues, concerns, and problems, with the hope that forewarned is forearmed. We hope you still are excited about conducting educational research. As you conduct it, we wish you the best. Remember, there are great opportunities for conducting research that might transform educational practice and make a dramatic difference in the quality of our schools and the quality of life experienced by our children.

References

Aronson, E., & Osherow, N. (1980). Cooperation, social behavior, and academic performance: Experiments in the desegregated classroom. In L. Bickman (Ed.), *Applied Social Psychology Annual* (Vol. 1, pp. 163-196). Beverly Hills, CA: Sage.

Berk, R. A., & Ray, S. C. (1982). Selection biases in sociological data. *Social Science Research, 11,* 352-398.

Boyer, E. L. (1983). *High school.* New York: Harper & Row.

Campbell, D. T. (1969). Reforms as experiments. *American Psychologist, 24,* 409-429.

Campbell, D. T., & Erlebacher, A. E. (1970). How regression artifacts in quasi-experimental evaluations can mistakenly make compensatory education look harmful. In J. Hellmuth (Ed.), *Compensatory education: A national debate. Vol. 3: Disadvantaged child* (pp. 185-210). New York: Brunner/Mazel.

Campbell, D. T., & Stanley, J. (1963). *Experimental and quasi-experimental designs for research.* Chicago: Rand McNally.

Carroll, J. M. (1990). The Copernican plan: Restructuring the American high school. *Phi Delta Kappan, 71*(5), 358-365.

Cohen, E. G. (1990). Continuing to cooperate: Prerequisites for success. *Phi Delta Kappan, 72*(2), 134-138.

Cook, T., & Campbell, D. T. (1979). *Quasi-experimentation.* Chicago: Rand McNally.

Cooper, H. M. (1989). *Integrating research: A guide for literature reviews* (2nd ed.). Newbury Park, CA: Sage.

Costner, H. L., & Schoenberg, R. (1973). Diagnosing indicator ills in multiple indicator models. In A. S. Goldberger & O. D. Duncan (Eds.), *Structural equation models in the social sciences* (pp. 167-199). New York: Seminar.

Cronbach, L. J., & Suppes, P. (1969). *Research for tomorrow's schools: Disciplined inquiry for education.* New York: Macmillan.

DeVellis, R. F. (1990). *Scale development: Theories and applications.* Newbury Park, CA: Sage.

Espin, C., Deno, S., Maruyama, G., & Cohen, C. (1989, March). *The Basic Academic Skills Samples (BASS): An instrument for the screening and identification of children at risk for failure in regular education classrooms.* Paper presented at the annual meeting of the American Educational Research Association, San Francisco.

Glass, G. (1976). Primary, secondary, and meta-analysis of research. *Educational Researcher, 5,* 3-8.

Glass, G. (1977). Integrating findings: The meta-analysis of research. *Review of Research in Education, 5,* 351-379.

Goodlad, J. I. (1984). *A place called school: Prospects for the future.* New York: McGraw-Hill.

Hall, G. E., George, A. A., & Rutherford, W. A. (1979). *Measuring stages of concern about the innovation: A manual for the use of the SoC Questionnaire.* Austin: University of Texas.

Hedrick, T., Bickman, L., & Rog, D. J. (in press). *Planning applied research.* Newbury Park, CA: Sage.

Henry, G. T. (1990). *Practical sampling.* Newbury Park, CA: Sage.

Hobbs, N. (Ed.). (1975). *Issues in the classification of children*. San Francisco: Jossey-Bass.

Homans, G. C. (1965). Group factors in worker productivity. In H. Proshansky & L. Seidenberg (Eds.), *Basic studies in social psychology* (pp. 592-604). New York: Holt.

Johnson, D. W., Johnson, R. T., & Maruyama, G. (1983). Interdependence and interpersonal attraction among heterogeneous individuals: A theoretical formulation and meta-analysis of the research. *Review of Educational Research, 53*, 5-54.

Johnson, D. W., Maruyama, G., Johnson, R. T., Nelson, D., & Skon, L. (1981). Effects of cooperative, competitive, and individualistic goal structures on achievement: A meta-analysis. *Psychological Bulletin, 89*, 47-62.

Jöreskog, K. G., & Sörbom, D. (1989). *LISREL 7: A guide to the program and applications*. Chicago: SPSS.

Judd, C. M., Smith, E., & Kidder, L. H. (1990). *Research methods in social relations* (6th ed.). New York: Holt, Rinehart & Winston.

Kenny, D. (1979). *Correlation and causality*. New York: John Wiley.

Lewin, K. (1946). Action research and minority problems. In K. Lewin (1948), *Resolving social conflicts: Selected papers on group dynamics* (pp. 201-216). New York: Harper.

Lipsey, M. (1990). *Design sensitivity: Statistical power for experimental research*. Newbury Park, CA: Sage.

Maruyama, G., Deno, S., Cohen, C., & Espin, C. (1989, March). *The School Characteristics Survey: An "effective school" based means of assessing learning environments*. Paper presented at the annual meeting of the American Educational Research Association, San Francisco.

Maruyama, G., & McGarvey, B. (1980). Evaluating causal models: An application of maximum likelihood analysis of structural equations. *Psychological Bulletin, 87*, 502-512.

McLaughlin, M. W. (1990). The Rand change agent study revisited: Macro perspectives and micro realities. *Educational Researcher, 19*(9), 11-16.

Miller, N., & Maruyama, G. (1975). Ordinal position and peer popularity. *Journal of Personality and Social Psychology, 34*, 615-624.

O'Sullivan, P. J., Ysseldyke, J. E., Christenson, S. L., & Thurlow, M. L. (1990). Mildly handicapped elementary students' opportunity to learn during reading instruction in mainstream and special education settings. *Reading Research Quarterly, 25*, 131-146.

Rosenthal, R. (1984). *Meta-analytic procedures for social research*. Newbury Park, CA: Sage.

Rosenthal, R., & Jacobson, L. (1968). *Pygmalion in the classroom: Teacher expectation and pupils' intellectual development*. New York: Holt, Rinehart & Winston.

Schanker, A. (1990). The end of the traditional model of schooling—and a proposal for using incentives to restructure our public schools. *Phi Delta Kappan, 71*(5), 345-357.

Schooler, C. (1972). Birth order effects: Not here, not now. *Psychological Bulletin, 78*, 161-175.

Shapiro, W. (1991, September). Education and tough choices. *Time*, 54-60.

Shulman, J. H. (1990). Now you see them, now you don't: Anonymity versus visibiilty in case studies of teachers. *Educational Researcher, 19*(6), 11-15.

Sieber, J. (1992). *Planning ethically responsible research: Developing an effective protocol*. Newbury Park, CA: Sage.

Solomon, D., Watson, M., Schaps, E., Battistich, V., & Solomon, J. (1990). Cooperative learning as part of a comprehensive classroom program designed to promote prosocial development. In S. Sharan (Ed.), *Cooperative learning: Theory and research* (pp. 231-260). New York: Praeger.

Thorndike, R. L. (1942). Regression fallacies in the matched groups experiment. *Psychometrika, 7,* 85-102.

Wahlstrom, K. S. (1990). School district decision making in the adoption of innovation. Unpublished doctoral dissertation, University of Minnesota. *Dissertation Abstracts International, 51,* 6:1868A, University Microfilms No. DA 9029716.

Winer, B. J. (1971). *Statistical principles in experimental design.* New York: McGraw-Hill.

Author Index

Subject Index

About the Authors

Geoffrey Maruyama is Professor of Educational Psychology, Adjunct Professor of Psychology, and Director of the Human Relations program within Educational Psychology at the University of Minnesota. He received his Ph.D. in social psychology from the University of Southern California. He has been a Spencer Foundation Fellow of the National Academy of Education and has received both a social issues dissertation award and the Gordon Allport Intergroup Relations Award from the Society for the Psychological Study of Social Issues (SPSSI). He has written in the areas of school achievement, school desegregation, cooperative learning, constructive ways of using controversy in schools, and structural equation methodologies. He has served on the American Psychological Association Committee for Ethnic Minority Human Resource Development and on the Council of Representatives of SPSSI.

Stanley Deno is Professor of Educational Psychology and head of the Special Education Program at the University of Minnesota. He received his Ph.D. in Educational Psychology at the University of Minnesota in 1965 and was on the faculty at the University of Delaware from 1965 to 1969. Since 1969 he has been actively involved at Minnesota in a wide range of school-based research projects funded by the federal government. Those projects address the development of effective special educational programs for students with disabilities. His most notable work has been in the development and use of data-based instructional methods, which led to the publication of a book entitled *Data-Based Program Modification*. In addition, he coauthored *Student Motivation and Classroom Management*. In 1982-1983, he was a Fulbright Scholar in Taiwan, and in 1991 he received the award from the Council for Exceptional Children for Outstanding Contributions to Teacher Education.

Applied Social Research Methods

$28.50 cloth
$13.95 paper

Place
Stamp
here

SAGE PUBLICATIONS, INC.
P.O. BOX 5084
NEWBURY PARK, CALIFORNIA 91359-9924